The Staghound

A VISUAL HISTORY OF THE T17E SERIES ARMORED CARS IN ALLIED SERVICE

by David Doyle

Published by Ampersand Publishing Company, Inc.
21 S.W. 1st Avenue, Delray Beach, Florida 33444

Acknowledgements:

Although my name appears as the author of this book, this project would not have been possible without the help of a number of other dedicated individuals. Reg Hodgson, whose vehicle appears on the cover, supplied many of the images, both photos of his superbly restored vehicle and period photos from his archive. The late Bart Vanderveen described Reg's Staghound as "probably the best" extant example. Furthermore, Reg acted as an intermediary, forwarding first-hand recollections of the men who fought in these vehicles. Reg also introduced me to Marco Hogenkamp, who has spent over a decade researching Staghounds in the meticulous manner of which only a professional engineer is capable. Marco enthusiastically and generously shared his knowledge and the fruits of his research. In addition, he provided me with photos of his own Staghound and from his archive, including those taken by his uncle during the war. Jesper Wilhelmsen and Flemming Hendriksen kindly provided photos and information concerning the Staghound III. The late Jacques Litttlefield and Michael Green gave me access to the rare T17E2 in storage at the Military Vehicle Technology Foundation.

Jim Gilmore traveled to the Military History Institute and copied rare factory photos for me when I could not. Don Moriarty did much the same at the Patton Museum. Scott Taylor generously shared photos of a Staghound preserved in Ottawa. Tom Kailbourn and Joe DeMarco shared their vast knowledge of armored vehicles and skillfully interpreted many of these photos for me. A special thanks to Denise, for patiently taking care of a host of things while I clambered about dusty vehicles and spent long, late hours at my desk and on the phone working on this project.

To all of these people, I am truly indebted.

Sources

A History of United States Armored Cars by John Hocking.
Office Chief of Ordnance, 1946.

Armored Car: A History of American Wheeled Combat Vehicles by R. P. Hunnicutt. Presidio Press, 2002.

Engineering Related to Wheeled and Half Track Vehicles or International Aid Requirements.
Chief of Ordnance-Detroit, 1945.

Wheels and Tracks 32: Staghound Armored Cars by Bart Vanderveen.
Battle of Britain Int. Ltd, 1990.

TM 9-741 Medium Armored Car T17E1.
War Department, 1942.

TM 9-1741C Ordnance Maintenance Chassis, Hull and Turret for Medium Armored Car T17E1.
War Department, 1943.

The Staghound in Canadian Service by Roger V. Lucy.
Service Publications, 2007.

©2009, Ampersand Publishing Company, Inc. All rights reserved. This publication may not be reproduced in part or in whole without written permission from the publisher, except in cases where quotations are needed for reviews.

Table of Contents

T17E1	5
T17E2	108
T17E3	115
Staghound II	117
Staghound III	119

Introduction

Although the U.S. Army conducted some experimental work on armored cars during the early 1930's, the general opinion within the army at that time was that there was no tactical need for such vehicles. Accordingly, OCM Item 13358, dated 14 January 1937, cancelled all specifications for armored cars. Only four years later, however, that opinion had changed.

In May 1941, the Armored Force Board concluded that the scout car then in use, the White M3A1, was not suitable for its intended purpose. The Board therefore recommended that a wheeled, turreted reconnaissance vehicle be procured as quickly as possible.

The Board's reversal of opinion was in part influenced by the British experience in the Middle East. There, at the onset of the North African Campaign against the Italians, British Troops used elderly Rolls Royce armored cars dating back to World War I with some success, despite their notable lack of firepower.

Almost concurrently, on 30 June 1941, the British Purchasing Commission forwarded their military characteristics for medium and heavy armored cars, vehicles for which they had an immediate need. On 11 July 1941, representatives from Technical Staff, Industrial Service, Armored Force and British Purchasing Commission held a conference at which a composite list of military characteristics was formulated that satisfied all parties. These characteristics for both medium and heavy armored cars were set forth on 17 July 1941. The medium armored car was designated the T17 and the heavy armored car the T18.

Leading automotive manufacturers were asked to submit proposals for pilot models of both the medium and heavy designs. Of the various proposals submitted, a 6-wheel design by the Ford Motor Co. and a 4-wheel design from the Chevrolet Division of General Motors Corporation showed the most promise. The decision was made to build one pilot model of each, and OCM Item 17217, dated 11 September 1941, approved this action and designated the Ford 6-wheel design as Armored Car T17 and the Chevrolet 4-wheel vehicle as Armored Car T17E1. This was an unusual departure from the normal nomenclature, in which the E suffix indicates a modification of the preceding number (in this case, T17).

Col. C. B. Bouchier of the British Army Staff kept a close eye on the development of the Armored Car T17 and T17E1. As early as September 1941, he made a trip to Detroit with an Ordnance Department representative to inspect the first wooden mock-ups of these vehicles and to discuss the design features with the automotive engineers. At this stage of development, it was assumed that either the T17 or T17E1 would be standardized for use by both the British and the U.S. Armored Force. However, in the early part of 1942 a decision was made to put both models in production, with the intention that the British would ultimately get the Armored Car T17E1 while U.S. forces would use the T17 version. This was a reasonable choice since the Armored Force favored the 6-wheel design while the British had enjoyed success with their own 4-wheeled Humber and Daimler armored cars. During the remainder of the development period, the British concentrated their interest on the Chevrolet T17E1 design, while also following the progress of the T17 model. It was at that time the policy of the Ordnance Department to build all combat vehicles to the requirements of the Armored Force even if they were earmarked for use by the British. This policy was based on the assumption that, because of supply problems, American troops engaged in a predominately British theater of operation would also use British-owned vehicles.

The designation M3A1E3 was applied to this main cavalry vehicle, armed with a 37mm gun, in November 1940. After initial testing with the 37mm gun mount T6, the vehicle was later re-equipped with the M25 37mm mount seen here. After testing, the M3A1E3 was determined to be unsatisfactory for its intended purpose, largely due to its excessive weight, high silhouette and inadequate protection. (NARA)

Armored Car T17

Ford Motor Co.'s proposal to build a single pilot model was approved on 10 October 1941. A second pilot model was added per OCM 17473, dated 27 November 1941.

As originally laid out, the T17 was powered by two 90 horsepower Ford engines and protected by face-hardened rolled armor plate. In the interest of standardization, however, on 26 October 1941 the Ordnance Department requested that Ford use the 110 horsepower Hercules JKD engines used in the Scout Car M3A1 and in Studebaker 2 1/2-ton trucks. To expedite production, the Ordnance Department approved the use of homogeneous armor plate and permitted welding of the plate on 16 February 1942.

The first pilot model was completed on 1 March 1942 and, beginning 14 March 1942, the vehicle was driven to Aberdeen Proving Ground for testing and demonstrations.

Even before completion of this first pilot, however, the decision had already been made to proceed with production of the Armored Car T17 for the Armored Command. A production contract for 2,260 vehicles was initiated on 30 January 1942. The production drawings were completed, and the Ford Motor Co. outfitted their St. Paul, Minnesota Branch to build them. Between March and September 1942, when the first production model was completed, the two pilot models underwent testing at General Motors Proving Ground, Armored Board at Fort Knox, Kentucky, and Aberdeen Proving Ground.

In the aftermath of the Pearl Harbor attack, U.S. arms procurement accelerated rapidly and contracts were issued for large numbers of unproven vehicles, many of them armored cars—for example, 1,000 T13 Trackless Tanks. Accordingly, on 14 October 1942 Brigadier General Williston Palmer convened the Special Armored Vehicle Board to sort through the various armored car projects then in the works, and then to test many of the prototypes. In a report dated 4 November 1942, the Board reported that the T17 was too heavy and bulky for practical use. Accordingly, the contract for the T17 was cut from 2,260 to 250 vehicles. Chief among the reasons to produce those 250 vehicles was the desire to keep the Ford plant busy until the Light Armored Car M8 could be put into production.

The British initially agreed to accept the 250 Armored Cars T17 through International Aid, and the vehicles were consequently modified to include brackets that met British stowage requirements. The vehicle was dubbed the Deerhound. However, a Service Board Test at the Desert Warfare Board for the British was conducted on six Armored Cars T17, and on the basis of that test the British decided that the vehicles were unsuited for their purposes. Once again without a home, the 37mm guns were removed from the vehicles for reuse, and the vehicles themselves assigned to Military Police Units in the United States. The T17 project was terminated as recorded in OCM 27818, dated 3 Feb 1944.

With the Armored Force dropping all requirements for a medium armored car, the door was open for the T17E1 to be totally adapted for British use. The vehicle was called the Staghound, and although some documents refer to the vehicle as the "Medium Armored Car, M6," the vehicle remained officially the T17E1.

Armored Car T17E1

The Chevrolet design proposed a 23,000-pound, 4x4 vehicle powered by two GMC 270 cubic inch engines, similar to those used in the CCKW, located behind the 37mm gun turret. Power steering and 14.00-20 combat tires provided the vehicle with the desired maneuverability. The Undersecretary of War approved Chevrolet's proposal to build one pilot vehicle at a cost of $75,000 on 11 October 1941. On 27 November 1941, authorization was granted to increase the procurement to two pilot models. Consequently, on 23 December 1941 the Chevrolet contract amount increased to $115,000 to include the second pilot vehicle.

In March 1942, Chevrolet delivered both pilot models to the Ordnance Department. The first vehicle went to General Motors Proving Ground for testing, and the second was driven overland to Aberdeen Proving Ground for a General Staff demonstration. Meanwhile, in January 1941, Chevrolet received an initial order for 2,000 production vehicles. Testing and research involving the pilot vehicles continued through October 1942, when Chevrolet's #2 Flint, Michigan plant delivered the first production vehicles.

Originally, the Armored Car T17E1 was designed for stowage equipment specified by the U.S. Armored Force. However, when it became apparent that the British would use the entire production run, the stowage arrangement was revised to accommodate their requirements. Armored Car T17E1 Issue Letter No. 2, dated 8 January 1943, describes this change.

At the request of the British Army Staff, a Desert Warfare Board test of the Armored Cars T17 and T17E1 was scheduled for 18 February 1943. This test proved the Armored Car T17E1 to be more mechanically reliable than the Armored Car T17, and helped justify the British decision to accept only the T17E1 vehicle.

Production of the T17E1 ended in December 1943.

Armored Car T17E2

On 1 June 1942, Col. C. B. Bouchier of the British Army Staff wrote to General J. K. Christmas to request that the Frazer-Nash twin .50 caliber turret, which Norge Division, Borg-Warner Corp. manufactured for British torpedo boats, be installed in an Armored Car T17E1 hull. The Ordnance Department immediately asked Chevrolet to make design studies of this installation and by 2 September 1942, the design studies had progressed sufficiently to issue RAD Order No. 218 for the installation of one turret in the pilot model of the Armored Car T17E1. Work on the development progressed rather slowly during October, November, and December 1942 due to the more urgent nature of the engineering work Chevrolet was simultaneously conducting on the Armored Cars T17E1 and T19E1. In January 1943, the British expressed a desire to have the last 500 Armored Cars T17E1 replaced by vehicles mounting the Frazer-Nash Turret.

The engineering work required for this installation proved to be much more extensive than was first indicated. A new turret race had to be designed and the turret basket had to be redesigned to accommodate the hydraulic pump and electric motor, which was a separate unit in the torpedo boat installation. In addition, turret armor had to be designed. The first pilot model was sent to Aberdeen Proving Ground and proof-fired from 23 to 26 March 1943. These tests indicated the need for a power booster ammunition feed and a better gunsight.

By this time, arrangements for production were already in place and every effort was being made to finalize the engineering as soon as possible. On 1 June 1943, a pilot model incorporating an ammunition feed booster and Navy Mk IX Sight was proof-fired at Erie Proving Ground in LaCarne, Ohio with complete success.

OCM Item 20645, dated 3 June 1943, designated the Armored Car T17E1 with the Norge Twin .50 caliber turret as the Armored Car T17E2.

In the spring of 1943 Brigadier G. M. Ross, Chief of the British Army Staff, A.F.V. office turned over the Armored Car T17E2 project to Lt. Col. J. N. Berkeley-Miller, who requested many minor design changes. Most of these changes concerned stowage arrangements that were easily revised without jeopardizing the initial production date. However, Col. Berkeley-Miller also expressed dissatisfaction with the turret rotation characteristic that was the same as that used for the British torpedo boat design. In order to alter the turret rotation characteristic to give the more

This T13 armored car, also known as the Trackless Tank, was photographed during testing at Aberdeen Proving Ground in November 1942. Virtually nothing about the T13 was conventional—it was intended to be, and was, a revolutionary vehicle with outstanding off-road performance. Its weight and mechanical complexity worked against it, however, and the project was terminated shortly after this photo was taken. (The Patton Museum)

sensitive creep speed control that he requested, considerable experimental work on the control valve was required. Although Issue Letter No. 3, dated 28 June 1943, released for production all other design features, it was not until 23 August 1943, in Issue Letter No. 9, that the control valve giving the desired turret rotation characteristic was released.

On 19 August 1943, Issue Letter No. 8 released an electric solenoid firing system to replace the very complex hydraulic system that had been carried over from the old design. A design check installation was made that was entirely satisfactory to the Ordnance Department—but not to Col. Berkeley-Miller. Since no agreement could be reached, Issue Letter No. 21, dated 28 October 1943, cancelled the solenoid firing, which did not appear in any production vehicle.

The first production pilot model was completed in September 1943 and was immediately sent to the Armored Board, Fort Knox, Kentucky, for testing. The results were quite satisfactory and indicated that only a few minor changes were necessary. These were incorporated in production and a true production model was sent for testing to the Anti-Aircraft Artillery Board, Camp Davis, North Carolina, in December 1943. This test was conducted to give the earliest possible reports of any field failures, but none developed.

Production of the T17E2 ended in early April 1944.

Armored Car T17E3

In September 1943, British field reports indicated the necessity of having a larger caliber gun on the Armored Car T17E1 that would be capable of firing effective HE shells to overcome roadblocks. British Army Staff representatives discussed the requirement with members of the Ordnance Department and although it was agreed that a 75mm gun would be most desirable, the necessity for speedy action dictated testing of a 75mm howitzer instead. Accordingly, the turret of a 75mm Howitzer Motor Carriage M8 was installed on a T17E1 hull. This conversion was eased by the fact that both vehicles used the same turret race.

The trial installation made in October 1943 proved successful, but Army Service Forces (ASF) approval could not be obtained for the production release until a proof-firing test was conducted. Proof-firing tests, witnessed by an ASF representative, were conducted on 9 December 1943 and were a complete success.

In the meantime, OCM Item 22278, dated 2 December 1943, had been passed, designating the vehicle as Armored Car T17E3 and requesting that a complete pilot model be produced for testing. This was never carried out, however, because the proof-firing test was accomplished by mounting a 75mm Howitzer Motor Carriage M8 production turret on an Armored Car T17E1 hull. It was believed that a complete pilot model with stowage and all details should not be manufactured unless ASF intended to approve production for the 100 vehicles that the British had requested. However, on 31 December 1943, Col. McInerney, Office of Chief of Ordnance, wrote a teletype to Office of Chief of Ordnance-Detroit with the information that ASF had informally stated that there would be no requirement for the Armored Car T17E3. Accordingly, the T17E3 project was cancelled.

Although factory production of all Staghound variants totaled a modest 3,844 vehicles of only two types—discounting the sole T17E3—once in service other variants were field produced that featured a variety of armament, or in some cases, no armament at all.

T17E1

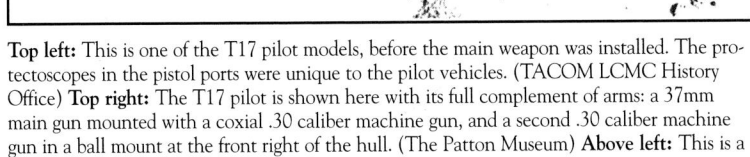

Top left: This is one of the T17 pilot models, before the main weapon was installed. The protectoscopes in the pistol ports were unique to the pilot vehicles. (TACOM LCMC History Office) **Top right:** The T17 pilot is shown here with its full complement of arms: a 37mm main gun mounted with a coxial .30 caliber machine gun, and a second .30 caliber machine gun in a ball mount at the front right of the hull. (The Patton Museum) **Above left:** This is a production vehicle being tested at Aberdeen Proving Ground in December 1942. Notice the reconfigured stowage compartments on top of the fenders, as well as the lack of protectoscopes in the pistol ports. The engine exhaust and air intakes also differ from those of the pilot vehicles. (The Patton Museum) **Above right:** The T17, through its transfer case, was capable of four- or six-wheel drive as conditions warranted. The twin Hercules JXD engines could push the machine up to 60 mph on road, but the vehicle's combat weight of 32,000 lbs resulted in a 13.8 horsepower per ton weight ratio and dismal off-road performance. (TACOM LCMC History Office)

This full-fledged production T17, registration number W-6025172, was tested at Fort Knox. Note the large stowage box between the first and second axles. (The Patton Museum)

The T17E1, popularly known as the Staghound, was much more successful than the Ford T17. Shown here is one of the Chevrolet prototypes. As with the Ford, the Chevrolet prototypes had protectoscopes in the turret pistol ports. The driver of the T17E1 could select either two- or four-wheel drive. (The Tank Museum, Bovington, Dorset)

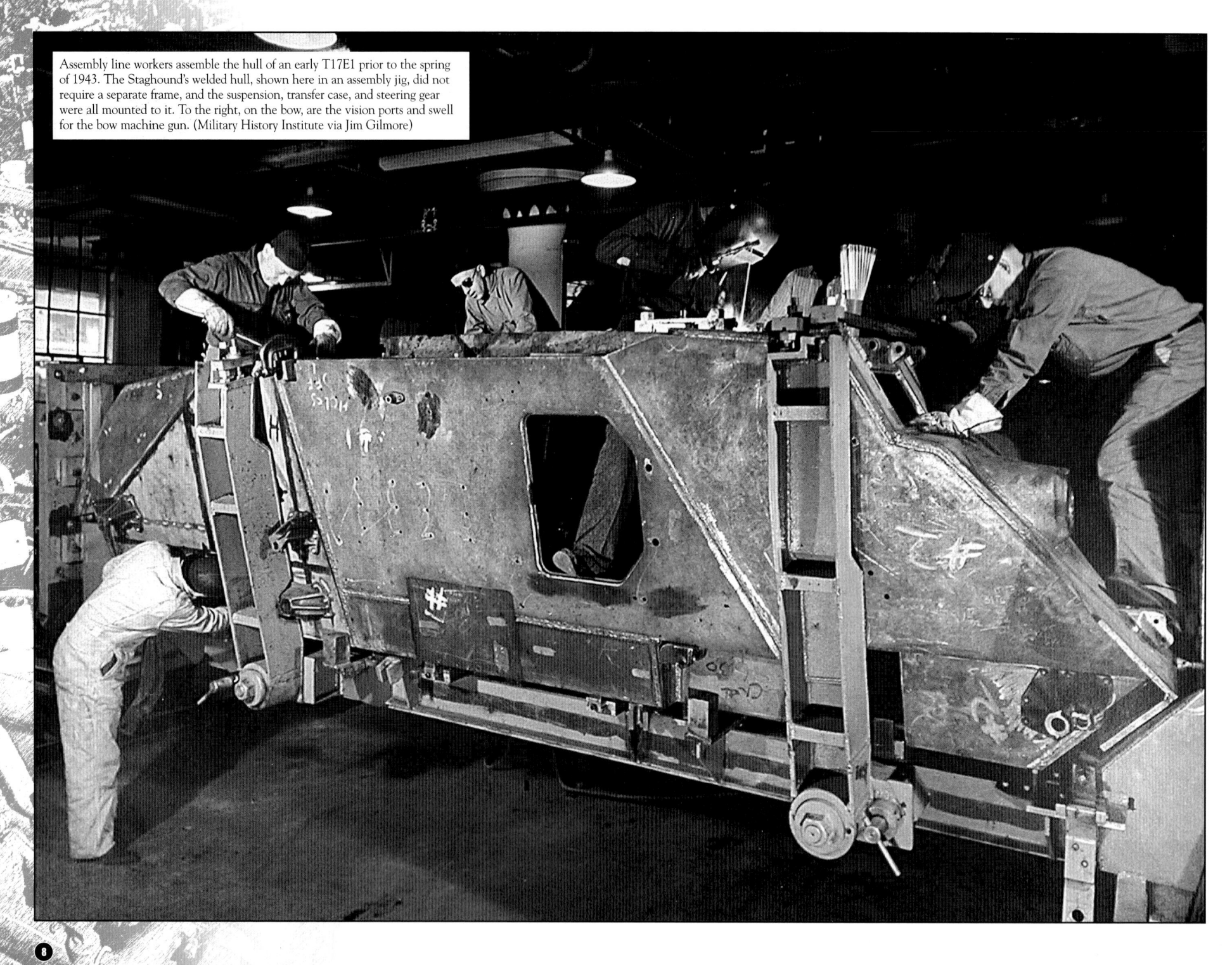

Assembly line workers assemble the hull of an early T17E1 prior to the spring of 1943. The Staghound's welded hull, shown here in an assembly jig, did not require a separate frame, and the suspension, transfer case, and steering gear were all mounted to it. To the right, on the bow, are the vision ports and swell for the bow machine gun. (Military History Institute via Jim Gilmore)

A hull is under construction sometime after May 1943, as indicated by the late-type headlight mounts. The front vision doors are installed, including their operating handles, which facilitated the opening of the doors from the outside. Welded diagonally on the glacis below the left vision door is a bracket for a tow cable. (Military History Institute via Jim Gilmore)

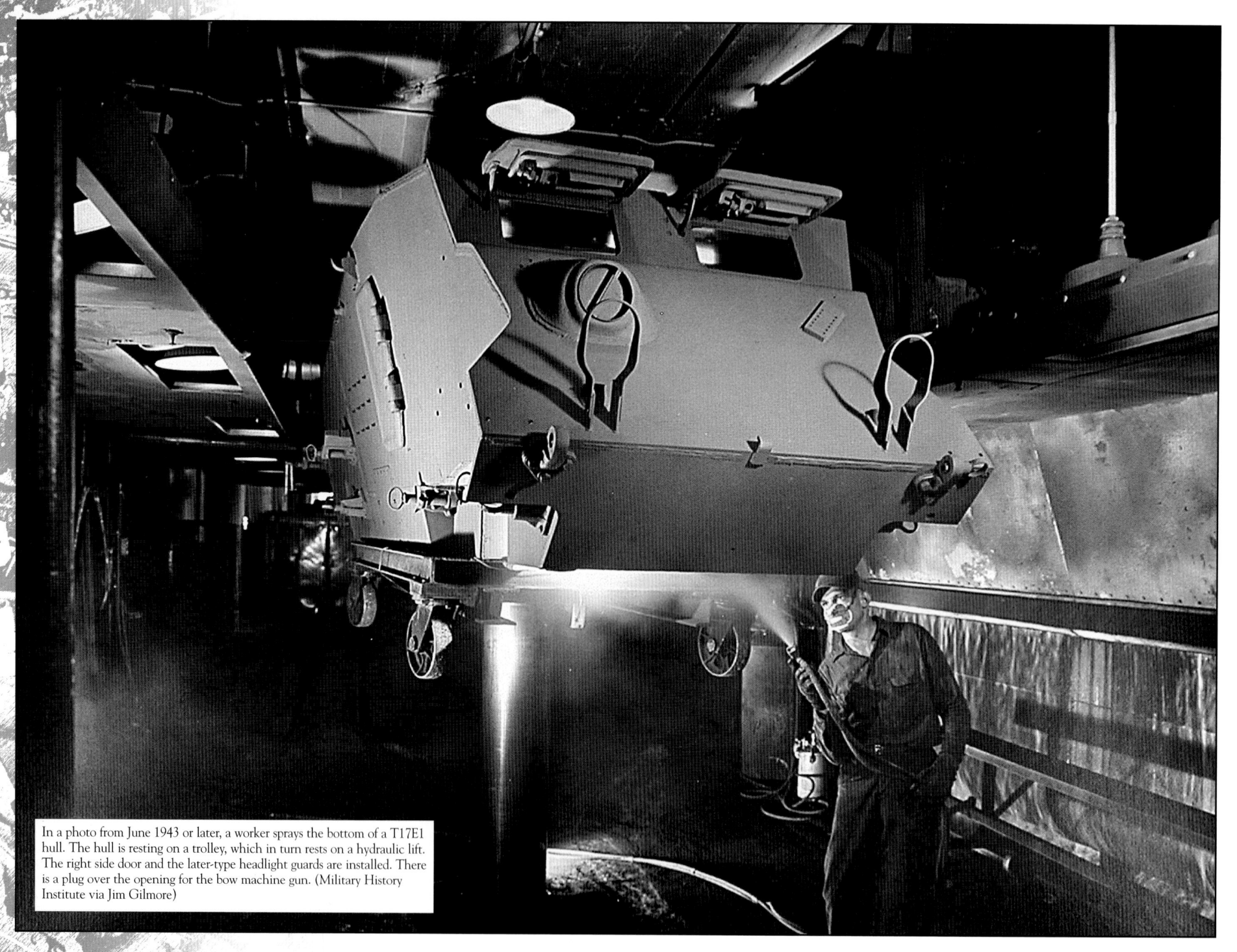

In a photo from June 1943 or later, a worker sprays the bottom of a T17E1 hull. The hull is resting on a trolley, which in turn rests on a hydraulic lift. The right side door and the later-type headlight guards are installed. There is a plug over the opening for the bow machine gun. (Military History Institute via Jim Gilmore)

A machinist is operating a milling machine to shape the opening for the gun mount in a turret casting. On the roof of the turret, to the front of the round opening for the gunner's periscope, is the opening for an M3 2" smoke mortar. This feature first appeared on the Staghound in May 1943. (Military History Institute via Jim Gilmore)

Welders work on the inside of a later-type T17E1 turret. Behind the workman and to his right is the opening for the M24A1 gun mount. To his left is the underside of the turret bustle. (Military History Institute via Jim Gilmore)

A welder assembles the parts of a T17E1 turret basket, held in place by a jig. On the floor around the basket are other, partially completed, baskets. Visible inside the basket to the right are clips for 37mm ammunition and a seat bracket. (Military History Institute via Jim Gilmore)

An array of Staghound axle assemblies awaits installation. These units, manufactured by Chevrolet, were full-floating, double-reduction type with 3.77:1 gear ratios. The front axles were designated model 3670077; the rear axles were 3670075. Visible at the ends of the axles are the hub and drum assemblies. (Military History Institute via Jim Gilmore)

Workmen ready a front axle complete with wheels and tires for installation on a Staghound hull. Already attached to the axle are the springs, shackles, and brake lines. Projecting up to the front of the worker at the right is a shock absorber link. (Military History Institute via Jim Gilmore)

Each Staghound was equipped with two Chevrolet 270 engines, which were based on the GMC engine design found in the CCKW 6x6 truck. They were six-cylinder, in-line, valve-in-head, and produced 194 horsepower. These engines, awaiting installation in a factory, are all left-hand units and are fitted with their transmissions and gear reduction assemblies. (Military History Institute via Jim Gilmore)

The Staghound's engines were arranged side by side, as seen in this view of the engine bay of an early (i.e., pre-June 1943) example with bolt-on engine covers. At the top are the radiators and radiator filler caps. At the bottom of the photograph are the cooling fans that draw air amidship through the radiators and exit downward out the rear of the engine compartment. Also visible are the engine ventilating air cleaners atop the valve covers and the water outlet lines alongside the valve covers. (Military History Institute via Jim Gilmore)

Workers in an assembly line pit make adjustments to service plates and drain plugs on the underside of a Staghound. The later-type headlight mounts mark this vehicle as one produced after May 1943. Details of the front springs, axle banjo, hub and drum assemblies, and tire tread pattern are in view. (Military History Institute via Jim Gilmore)

In this view of the rear of the fighting compartment of an early Staghound with the turret removed, the twin fixed fire extinguishers are at the center. Oil-bath air cleaners are on either side of the top of the bulkhead, and Hydrovacs are below them. At the bottom of the photo is the transfer case. The box-shaped tunnel for the rear propeller shaft was later changed to a rounded shape. 37mm ammunition clips have not been installed on the bulkhead. (Military History Institute via Jim Gilmore)

To the left of this turret basket, on which the turret has not yet been installed, are the turret lock (white T-handle) and powered traversing controls. At the bottom is the 24-volt electric motor with the turret hydraulic pump mounted on the end. The loader/wireless operator's seat is on top of the ammunition and smoke bomb storage bin. Below is the storage place for two hand grenade boxes. (Military History Institute via Jim Gilmore)

Left: A row of Staghounds on an assembly line are fairly early examples, as indicated by their headlight mounts and the M24 gun mount with the rounded shield on the lead vehicle. **Right:** A turret with an M24A1 gun mount with a boxy shield is being lowered onto a later (post-May 1943) T17E1. Unlike the earlier Staghounds in the left-hand photo, those in this image have side plates that extend about 30mm above the hull roof to protect the turret bearing. The fenders were attached to the hull near the end of the manufacturing process. (Military History Institute via Jim Gilmore)

Female workers at a tank depot apply sealant and non-hygroscopic tape to prepare a later Staghound for overseas shipment. Plugs are inserted into the sockets for the headlights, and a wooden support has been installed below the 37mm gun barrel. A waterproof cover has been fitted over the M24A1 gun mount. (Military History Institute via Jim Gilmore)

Left: Technicians wrestle a No. 19 wireless set up to the turret during the final detailing of a Staghound at a tank depot. At the bottom is a later-type 37-gallon jettisonable fuel tank.
Right: A view of the driver's compartment from behind the right seat. To the left of the driver's head are carburetor choke levers and hand throttles. The instrument panel has transmission oil pressure warning lights, indicating a date of acceptance after March 1943. To the front of the driver's head is a periscope holder. Storage racks for .30 caliber ammunition boxes were mounted between the driver and co-driver on the tunnel of production Staghounds. (Military History Institute via Jim Gilmore)

This Staghound, registration number USA-6023720, was photographed in late May 1943 ready for overseas shipment, with sealant applied and spare-parts crates strapped down. The vehicle had hinged engine decks, 37-gallon jettisonable fuel tanks, and a mount for a sun-compass on the turret. The storage box under the left fuel tank held blanket rolls, a collapsible bucket, C-rations, a tire pump and other oddments. (Military History Institute via Jim Gilmore)

Early Staghounds are being secured for shipment on Norfolk & Western flatcars. All have the bolt-down engine decks and early-type rear lifting eyes. To protect the turret bearing during shipment, the vehicles have been modified by welding a tubular section of steel on top of the side armor plate next to the turret, a feature seen on some Staghounds in Australian service. The right-side storage box under the jettisonable fuel tanks was designated a luggage box. (Military History Institute via Jim Gilmore)

A line of Staghounds with M24A1 gun mounts and late-type 37-gallon jettisonable fuel tanks and headlight mounts are being prepared on flatcars for overseas shipment circa late July 1943. The lead vehicle wears both British War Department and U.S. registration numbers, F116443 and USA-6024258 respectively. (Military History Institute via Jim Gilmore)

A workman secures another Staghound in the same consignment as the preceding photograph. Note the rolled outer edges of the fenders. Metal strapping material has been used to secure the barrels to wooden blocks, holding them firmly in place for transit. (Military History Institute via Jim Gilmore)

This T17E1, registration number USA-6024839, was photographed at Aberdeen Proving Ground on 4 December 1942. It was the second production vehicle, accepted into U.S. inventory in October 1942. Note the pistol port on the side of the turret, which lacks a protectoscope vision device. Other features are the M24 gun mount and early-style, rubber-covered, 25-gallon jettisonable fuel tanks. A muzzle cover is fitted on the 37mm gun. (The Patton Museum via Don Moriarty)

In this three-quarters left-rear view of the second production T17E1, a shovel and machine gun tripod are secured to the rear side of the hull. The U-shaped steps at the rear of the vehicle are bolted to the hull, not welded. This was standard practice on early Staghounds. Note the taillight and guard on the side of the rear hull overhang. (Reg Hodgson Collection)

This overhead view of the second production T17E1 evinces several features of early-production vehicles, including the bolt-down engine covers and the hull side plates that come flush with the roof in the area next to the turret, unlike the hinged engine covers and raised side panels of later vehicles. This example also lacks the smoke grenade launcher aperture, spotlight, and mount for a .30 caliber machine gun found on later Staghounds. (The Patton Museum via Don Moriarty)

In this factory photo of an early T17E1 (or possibly a T17) turret and turret basket, a pistol port with protectoscope is installed on the side of the turret. The lifting eyes were screwed into threaded sockets; when not in use, the eyes were removed and the sockets protected by plugs. Visible through the opening in the basket are the loader's seat; and on the floor is the 24-volt electric motor on which the turret traversing hydraulic pump is mounted. (Military History Institute via Jim Gilmore)

A variety of early and late Staghounds are parked at a depot in the United Kingdom, probably before D-day. The closest vehicle (with part of the turret showing at the bottom left) and the fourth one in line are later examples, with machine gun pedestals on the turret and, visible on the fourth vehicle, folding rear lifting eyes and hinged engine covers. The second and third Staghounds have bolt-down engine covers and welded-shut pistol ports without protectoscopes on the turrets. (The Tank Museum, Bovington, Dorset)

A very early Staghound, with welded-shut pistol ports on its turret and a M24 gun mount. This vehicle features a commander's hatch that is hinged to the front instead of on the outer sides, a configuration common on Staghounds in Polish and New Zealand service. Note the mounting plate for British 4" smoke dischargers on the right rear side of the turret. The front fenders have holes cut in them to accommodate ammunition boxes. Standard British parabolic rearview mirrors have been mounted on the front of the vehicle. (The Tank Museum, Bovington, Dorset)

In another photo of the same Staghound, a mount for a .30 caliber machine gun has been welded to the left side of the turret. Above "Link 1 of 1," painted in white on the side above the crew door, is the siren. The U.S. registration number indicates that this Staghound was produced in late January 1943 from contract DA-W-374-ORD-281, Production Order T-3288. The early, 25-gallon jettisonable fuel tanks are identifiable by their rubber covers and lifting straps on each end, in contrast to the uncovered steel of the later 37-gallon tanks. (The Tank Museum, Bovington, Dorset)

Early Staghounds in Polish service are tightly parked on a street in Italy. As field modifications, pedestal mounts for .30-caliber machine guns have been welded to the left rear of the turret roofs. Additionally, the commander's hatches have been converted to the front-hinged type and have had their periscopes removed. A hold-open brace has been installed to the side of the loader's hatch and racks for liquid containers have been mounted on the rear fenders. The tires are highway tread instead of the much more common non-directional tread. (NARA)

An Australian Staghound bears a hard edge camouflage scheme. Australian Staghounds kept the original U.S. registration numbers, although usually without the "USA" prefix. This early-production vehicle has the M24 gun mount. (The Tank Museum, Bovington, Dorset)

The jettisonable fuel tanks have been removed from this early Staghound, revealing details of the drop tank mount. These tanks were above the level of the internal, 62-gallon main fuel tank into which they discharged their contents by gravity. When jettisoned, the tanks rolled down the curved mounts. The vehicle bears a British war department (WD) number, commonly referred to as a census number, retained by the Canadian army. The letter F indicates an armored car. It was photographed at the Canadian army receiving unit in the United Kingdom prior to D-day. (Library and Archives Canada)

A right-rear three-quarter view of the same Staghound shown in the preceding photo. Note the layout of the mufflers on the rear overhang and the grab handles, radiator filler covers and crankcase filler tube covers on the two-piece, bolt-down engine cover. The U-shaped rear lifting eyes of the early Staghounds were later replaced by a fold-down type. (Library and Archives Canada)

A roll of camouflage netting is draped on the front of this early-production Canadian Staghound I with a M24 gun mount photographed in San Vito Chietino, Italy on 15 February 1944. Faintly visible just above the ammunition box mounted to the left front fender is the insignia of the 1st Canadian Corps. The cover for the vision slot in the driver's forward-vision door has been opened, providing direct forward vision without having to open the entire door. Stored over the jettisonable fuel tank are the barrel cleaning rods. (Library and Archives Canada)

Photographed during field maneuvers in England in late December 1943, this Staghound wears the insignia of D Squadron, 12th Manitoba Dragoons. The fixture set at an angle below the driver's forward vision port was a mounting for an adjustable tow cable bracket, used to secure the heavy wire tow rope. (Library and Archives Canada)

A frontal view of the same Staghound reveals more details of the unit markings. The early-style headlight mounts are visible. Note the "191" within the upward-pointing lazy 2nd Canadian Corps. The Canadian maple leaf was either Gold or more commonly yellow on a blue diamond for the 2nd Canadian Corps. The diamond was mounted on the red/white/red background. This red/white/red background was a marking used on British armor to indicate armored vehicles. "191" was the troop number and was also used as the radio call sign. The driver's vision port has been fitted with a removable glass windshield with inner and outer windshield wipers. (Library and Archives Canada)

Preceded by a Canadian Provost (military police) soldier on a motorcycle, a Staghound passes the reviewing stand during an end-of-war parade in Utrecht, Holland in 1945. (Library and Archives Canada)

Photographed at the General Motors Proving Ground on 10 June 1943, this late production T17E1 bore the U.S. Army registration number 6023735 and ordnance serial number 902. On this variant the pistol ports have been deleted from the turret and the M24A1 gun mount, with its angular gun shield, has superseded the M24 mount. The approximately 30mm upward extension of the side armor, a characteristic feature of later Staghounds, is apparent where the extension steps down next to the engine air intake shroud behind the turret. (The Patton Museum via Don Moriarty)

A rear view of the same T17E1 shown in the preceding photo reveals the hinges of the engine covers and the fold-down lifting eyes typical of later Staghounds. A storage box for tire chains has been mounted between the mufflers. (The Patton Museum via Don Moriarty)

A driver and assistant driver peer through removable windshields in a late production T17E1. Note the manner in which the operating arms of the vision doors protrude through oblong holes in the frontal armor. The gun mount is the M24A1, which included as a gunsight a M4 periscope with a M40 sighting telescope mounted inside the M4 periscope. (Military History Institute via Jim Gilmore)

On the upper left side of the turret of this late production Staghound is a mounting bracket for a sun compass, a device similar to a sundial that could be used as a rough navigation aid. Mounted on the turret roof is a spotlight. The armored flaps on the front vision doors are partially raised. (Military History Institute via Jim Gilmore)

The jettisonable fuel tank is the late, 37-gallon version; note the raised ridges on the surface next to the hold-down straps. Next to the side of the air intake shroud behind the turret, the stepped shape of the 30mm raised extension of the side armor, which protects the turret bearing, is particularly prominent. Note also the large hinges of the engine covers and the welded-on step at the rear of the hull. (Military History Institute via Jim Gilmore)

Details of the mufflers and muffler flanges. A metal strap held the body of each muffler in place, while the flanges were bolted to the hull. Above the box between the mufflers is the hinged cover for the main fuel tank filler. (Military History Institute via Jim Gilmore)

A trio of late production Staghounds is deployed in a field. They have the late model jettisonable fuel tanks—the slightly protruding rims are a visual identifier. The .30 caliber machine guns are not installed in the ball mounts. Tags with numbers are hanging from the headlight guards of the vehicle to the left. (Military History Institute via Jim Gilmore)

This early Staghound, registration number USA-6024950, accepted in December 1942, has been retrofitted with features common on late production vehicles including hinged engine covers, a M24A1 gun mount, 37-gallon jettisonable fuel tanks and a mount for a sun compass on the forward upper right side of the turret. The vehicle has a full complement of pioneer tools and stowed equipment, including the two-part barrel cleaning rod for the 37mm gun above the jettisonable fuel tank. (The Patton Museum)

The lack of a top extension on the side plates of the hull is a key indication that this vehicle is an early Staghound. Other retrofitted late production features include a .30 caliber machine gun pedestal mount at the rear of the turret and a spotlight on its roof. Stored in a protective sleeve over the right jettisonable fuel tank are antenna sections. (The Patton Museum via Don Moriarty)

In this frontal view of the same retrofitted Staghound, note the casting number below the periscope port in the M24A1 gun mount and the method used to secure the tow cable to the tow clevises and the brackets. The spring shackles are visible behind the cutouts on the sides of the lower front hull plate. (The Patton Museum via Don Moriarty)

Many features of the upper surfaces of the Staghound are evident in this overhead view of the retrofitted vehicle, including the five rotating periscope mounts, the casting mounts to the front of the turret hatches, the opening for the smoke mortar and the sun compass bracket to the side of the gunner's periscope. (The Patton Museum via Don Moriarty)

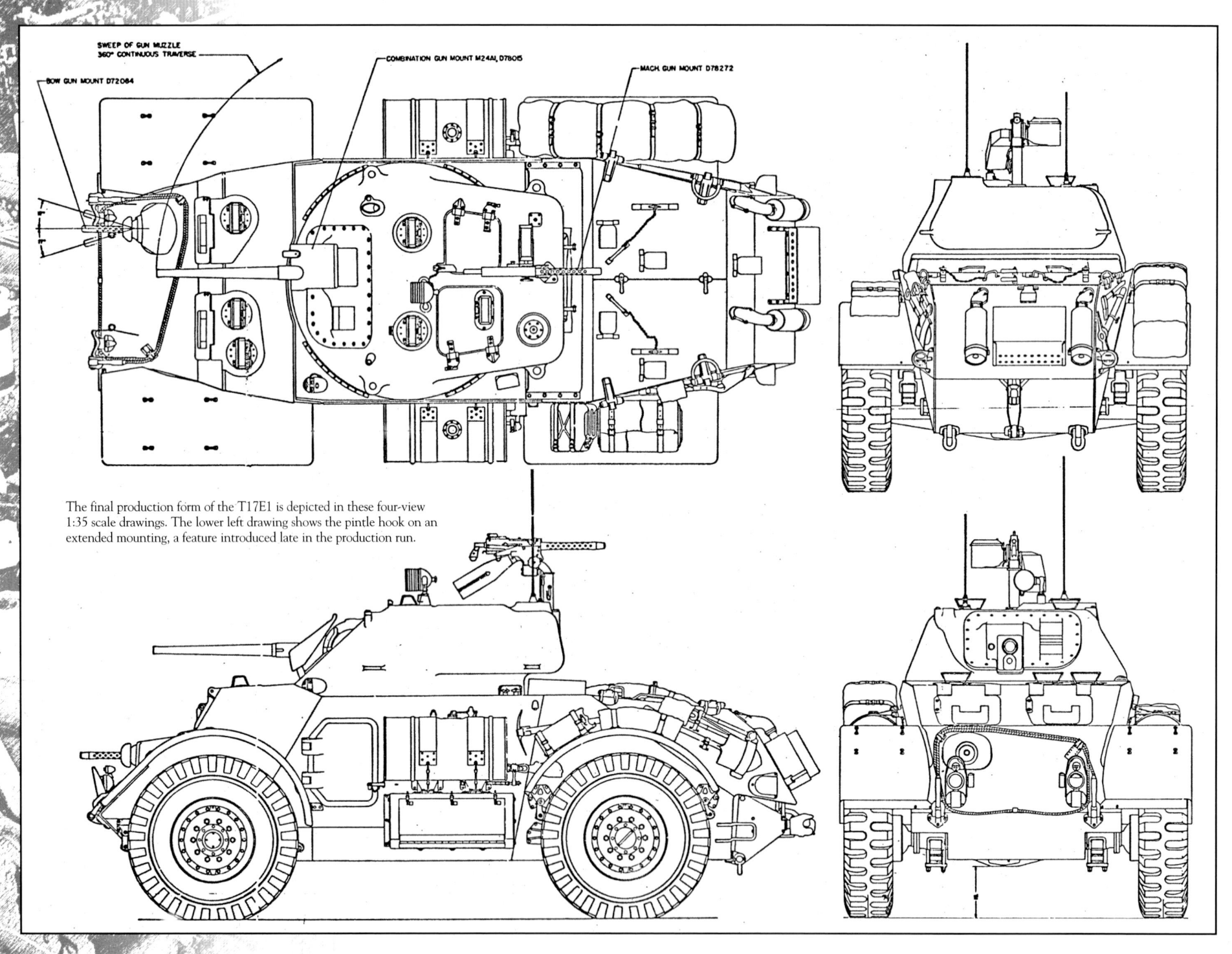

The final production form of the T17E1 is depicted in these four-view 1:35 scale drawings. The lower left drawing shows the pintle hook on an extended mounting, a feature introduced late in the production run.

Later-model Staghounds of A Squadron, 12th Manitoba Dragoons, advance down a railroad grade in the Hochwald Forest, Germany, on 2 March 1945 just after British engineers pulled up the railway tracks. The lead vehicle has chains on all its tires, while the second has them on the rear tires only. Note the equipment rack in lieu of the jettisonable fuel tank, a feature often found on Canadian Staghounds. (Library and Archives Canada)

A Staghound of the 6 Brigade, 2nd Division Maisonneuve Regiment passes a knocked out Tiger II on the road to Vimoutiers, near Billot, France on 22 August 1944. The boxes with grilles on the rear fender are part of the four-foot deep-water fording kit. This kit proved to be redundant, since the regiment had a dry landing on the beach at Normandy. The boxes were often left in place, both because it was laborious to remove them and because they minimized the blowing of dusty exhaust air from the engine compartment. (Library and Archives Canada)

Late production Staghounds of B Squadron, 12th Manitoba Dragoons, cross the Seine River at Elbeuf, France on 28 August 1944. Stored equipment on the lead vehicle includes ammunition boxes on the front fenders, helmets and a jumble of tarps and bedrolls. (Library and Archives Canada)

Troopers remove railroad ties from the engine deck of a late Staghound of the 12th Manitoba Dragoons, and lay them down to make a smoother approach to the pontoon bridge at Elbeuf on 28 August 1944. Camouflage netting is draped over the turret. A storage bin fabricated from tubing and wire mesh occupies the space previously dedicated to the jettisonable fuel tanks; this was a Canadian innovation. (Library and Archives Canada)

Staghounds, probably from a British or Polish unit, drive by a scout car and German POWs in northwest Europe in early 1945. The lead vehicle has been fitted with a large storage box with a hinged cover and a white Allied star painted on its side. Note the tripod-type stand for the rearview mirror on the fender. (Imperial War Museum)

In September 1944 this Staghound of the 12th Manitoba Dragoons was photographed in Blankenberge, Belgium during operations of the First Canadian Army to secure the coast of that country. A "14" bridge-classification marking is below the registration number, and a simple rack for holding stowed gear is above the storage box between the fenders. (Library and Archives Canada)

A late Staghound of B Squadron, 12th Manitoba Dragoons, follows a Universal Carrier in the Hochwald Forest, Germany, in March 1945. The regiment was heavily engaged in the drive to capture the Hochwald Gap early that month, preparatory to the Rhine River crossings. (Library and Archives of Canada)

Another view of the same Universal Carrier and Staghounds of B Squadron, 12th Manitoba Dragoons, in the Hochwald Forest. The "101" in the square above the registration number stands for 10th Troop, 1st car. Note the placement of the ammunition boxes on top of the front fenders. (Library and Archives Canada)

Commonwealth Staghounds, probably from the 12th Manitoba Dragoons, pass a group of German POWs in northwest Germany in April or May 1945. The white "44" superimposed on a blue/green square signifies a British or Commonwealth reconnaissance vehicle belonging to an armored car regiment. Visible on the rear fenders are the mountings for the deep-water fording kit. Note the "V" type aerial that often indicated a command Staghound. (Imperial War Museum)

A grime-covered Staghound I from the 2nd New Zealand Division's Divisional Cavalry Regiment passes civilians on a road somewhere in Italy. A dust cover is fitted over the top of the shield of the M24A1 gun mount, and knapsacks and bedrolls are secured to virtually every available space. (Imperial War Museum)

A Staghound from contract W-374-ORD-1315, production order T-3795 (accepted in July or August 1943), was photographed at a depot the United Kingdom on 19 March 1944. The vehicle, which was later assigned to the 12th Manitoba Dragoons, does not have hatch locks installed on the hinges of the turret hatches, a feature which became a standard factory installation in August 1943. The slightly raised profile of the commander's hatch is evident from this angle. (Library and Archives Canada)

A rear view of the same vehicle reveals that it has been fitted with a pintle hook on an extended mount below the rear overhang of the upper hull. The box with the vehicle registration number was actually a bin with no lid used for stowing tire chains. (Library and Archives Canada)

Photographed in Zeddam, Holland on 4 April 1945, this late Staghound of A Squadron, 12th Manitoba Dragoons, has been converted to a communications, or rear-link, vehicle by removing the guns from the M24A1 gun mount and installing a CR-229 radio, which had a range of 125 miles. This vehicle was intended to provide a radio link between the regiment and its parent unit, either division or corps. (Library and Archives Canada)

Crewmen pose on the same rear-link Staghound at Zeddam, including an RAF pilot sitting on the turret wearing flying boots and a shearling jacket. It is possible that he was a forward observer. The British developed two other special types of radio cars based on the Staghound: the command version, recognizable by the removal of the main armament and bow machine gun; and the control version, which retained the main armament and added an equipment box to the rear of the turret. (Library and Archives Canada)

Lieutenant General Guy Simonds, commander of 2nd Canadian Corps, poses in his specially modified Staghound convertible, dubbed "Charger," during the crossing of the Seine at Elbeuf, France on 28 August 1944. The vehicle was converted in Normandy in late July of that year by removing the turret and part of the upper hull and installing a windshield and canvas top, which is folded at the rear of the crew compartment. Part of the fording kit is still attached to the rear fender. (Library and Archives Canada)

In April 1945 the Canadian Army experimented with an eight-round rocket launcher mounted on the turret of a Staghound from 1st Canadian Armoured Corps Reinforcement Unit. The rockets had a 5" warhead weighing 29 pounds and were of the same type used in the Canadian Land Mattress rocket-launcher system. (Library and Archives Canada)

The launcher and the 37mm main gun elevated simultaneously by means of a link attached to the gun shield and the launcher. During tests, back-blast from the rockets crumpled the rear fender. Note that the tire-chain bin is installed above the jettisonable fuel tank mounts instead of between the mufflers. (Library and Archives Canada)

The No. 1 Canadian Base Workshop mounted the launcher on the Staghound. The right rear fender was also battered during testing. Note the ignition wires for the rockets. (Library and Archives Canada)

A rocket has just been launched from the Staghound during tests. Both the elevating link and the strut welded to the gun shield to which that link is attached are visible. The British continued testing this weapon system for almost a year after the end of the war. (Library and Archives Canada)

In this photograph from 14 February 1944, D Squadron, 12th Manitoba Dragoons, conduct tests with a Staghound fitted with two 12' aluminum bridging trestles for crossing trenches and other obstacles. The trestles rested on the fenders and brackets fitted above the side stowage boxes. The tests were a success, and the regiment outfitted one Staghound per troop to carry the trestles. The Royal Canadian Dragoons used them as well. (Library and Archives Canada)

Staghounds of B Squadron, 12th Manitoba Dragoons, participate in a parade in Amsterdam, Holland on 28 June 1945. In the background are Staghounds of C Squadron. The vehicle in the right foreground is an earlier variant with a M24 gun mount, while the rest are later vehicles equipped with the M24A1 mount. (Library and Archives Canada)

Late production features visible on this T17E1 Staghound, restored by Marco Hogenkamp, include the .30 caliber machine gun mount and the spotlight on the turret roof, the M24A1 gun mount, the lack of a pistol port in the turret, and the stepped extension at the top of the welded seam of the rear and center plates. (Marco Hogenkamp)

Top left: This headlight mount is an early production type. **Top right:** On the turret top, left to right, are a British Cole sun compass Mk III, periscope mount, spotlight and cap for the spotlight socket. This type of sun compass was not found on Staghounds in wartime Europe. **Above left:** A close-up view of the mount for a split, or V-shaped, wireless antenna at the right rear of the turret. Note the raised rim around the commander's hatch. **Above right:** The left rear of the hull. Note the stowed M2 tripod for a Browning M1919A4 machine gun and the Canadian shovel. The shovel does not fit in the bracket, which was designed for an American tool. (Marco Hogenkamp)

A restored Staghound bears the markings of 2nd Canadian Corps. The registration number is painted on the tire-chain box between the mufflers. Knapsacks are draped over the turret bustle. This vehicle lacks the towing pintle. (Army Motors)

Top left: Above the tire-chain box between the mufflers is the filler cover for the main fuel tank. **Top right:** The rear steps on this vehicle were bent parallel to the rear of the vehicle to accommodate the 4' deep-water fording kit. **Above left and right:** The steps were welded to the hull. Also visible is the guard for the taillight. (Marco Hogenkamp)

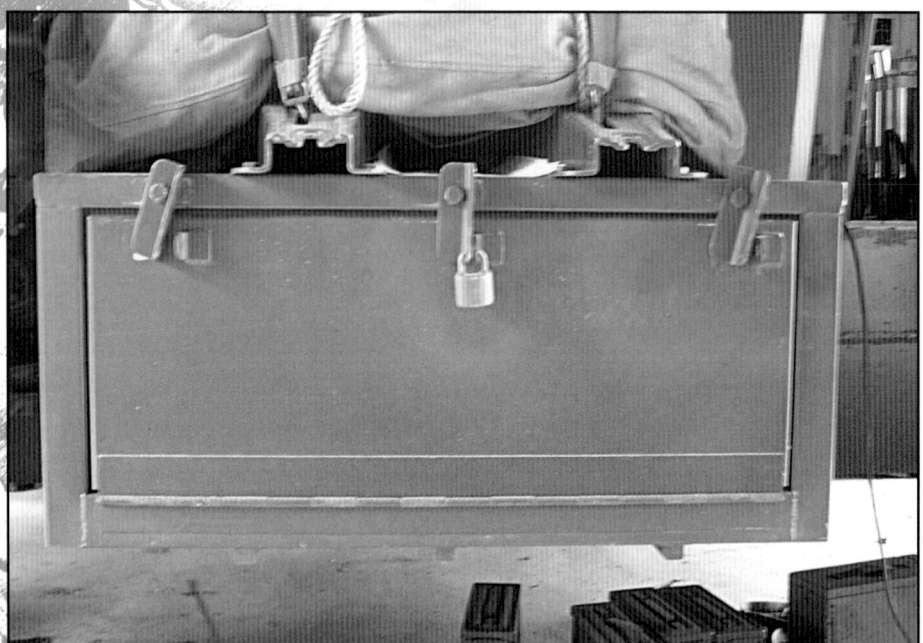

Top left: Typical tires for the Staghound were 12-ply 14.00-20. The wheels were combat rims. **Top right:** A detail shot of the welded seam between the left rear and center hull plates. Note the air intake cover, the extended center armor plate and the hole to drain water buildup on the hull roof. **Above left:** The stowage box held heavy tools, the jack and the air compressor. Simple toggles secured the door. **Above right:** The front right wheel and tire with non-directional tread. (Marco Hogenkamp)

This late production Staghound, owned and restored by Reg Hodgson, bears the markings the 12th Manitoba Dragoons and the 2nd Canadian Corps. This example has the tire chain box mounted at the center of the hull side. A roll is strapped to footman loops on the box. (Reg Hodgson)

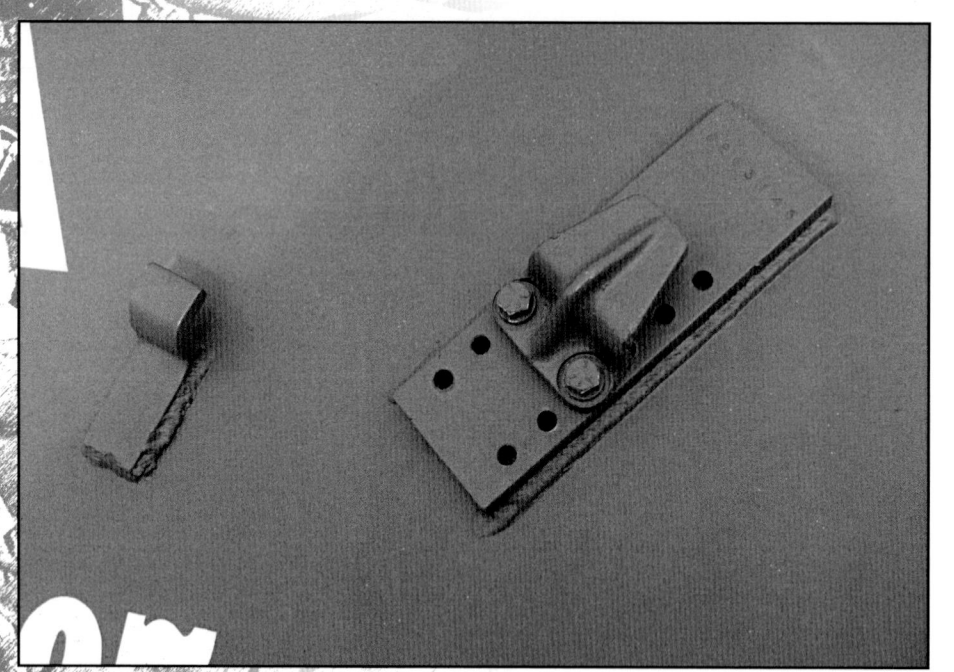

Top left: The forward vision doors and the vision-slit covers are in the open position. **Top right:** Note the locking latch inside this door. **Above left:** The adjustable tow cable bracket below the driver's vision door. **Above right:** Two extra cable brackets, a wartime British and Canadian modification, believed to hold concertina wire, are welded to the front hull plate. (Reg Hodgson)

Left: Atop the service headlights are blackout marker lamps. Cotter pins retaining the towing clevis are visible. **Right:** The cylindrical late-type headlight mount and the mount for the headlight brush guard are welded to the bow of the hull. A protective canvas sleeve covers the bow machine gun. (Reg Hodgson)

The vision-slit covers of the open forward-vision doors are in the raised position, revealing the wide and very narrow vision slits in the recesses. When the vision doors were closed during combat, the driver and assistant driver could get a forward view using the slits and the periscopes. On the rearview mirror support is the charging buffalo, non-official emblem of the 18th Armoured Car Regiment (12th Manitoba Dragoons). (Reg Hodgson)

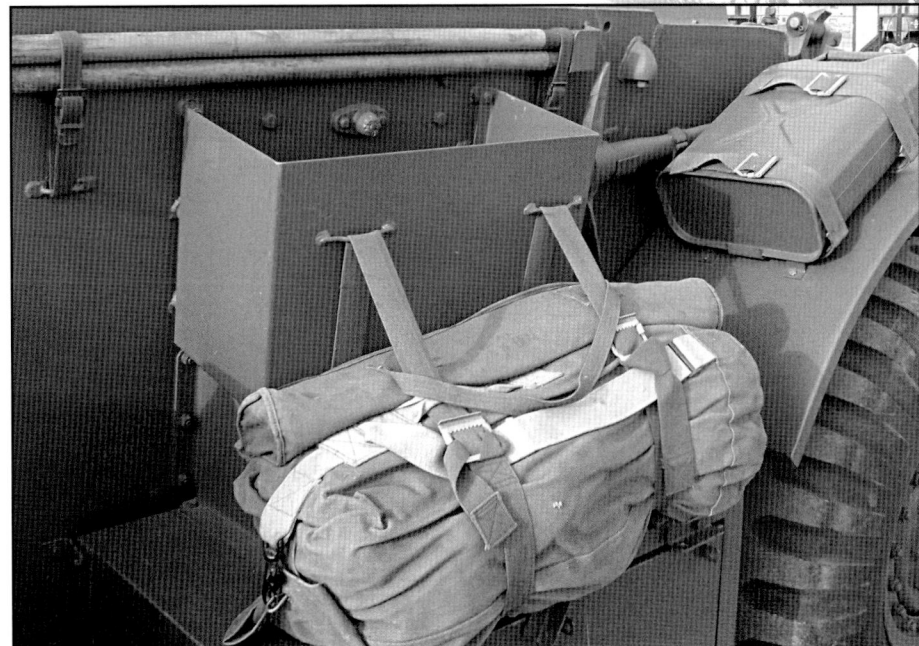

Top left and right: The warning siren is mounted on the left front of the hull roof, and is operated by a foot button below the steering column. **Above left:** The inside of both entry doors has provisions for storing a box of .30 caliber ammunition. Note the door latch. **Above right:** Between the left fenders are the barrel cleaning rods, tire chain box and liquid container. (Reg Hodgson)

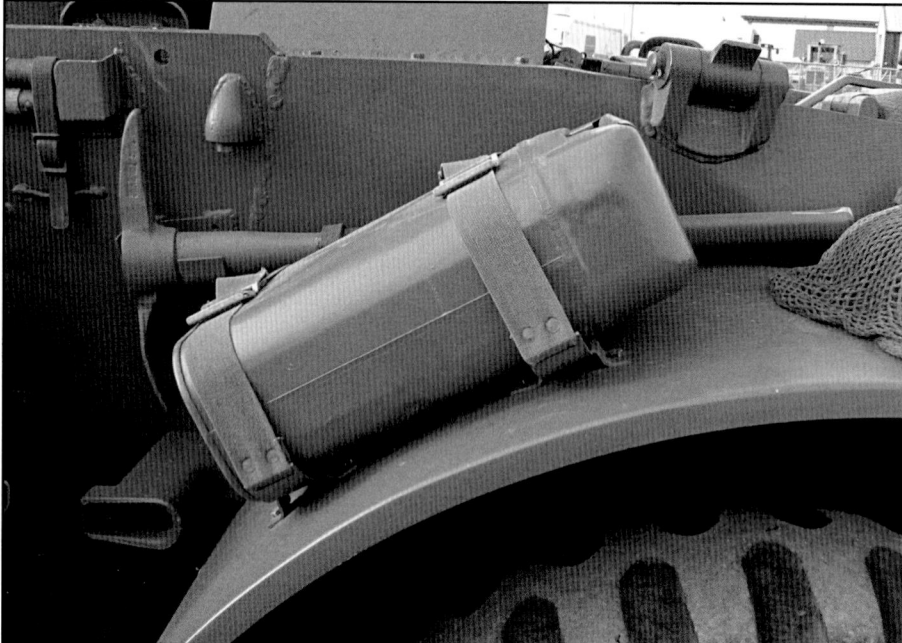

Top left: Part of the turret basket is visible through the side door. **Top right:** The liquid fuel container is secured to the rear fender by webbing straps through footman loops. **Above left:** Arrayed on the hinged engine covers are the covers for the radiator and crankcase oil filler tubes and the grab handles. The sand channel brackets and clamps—the bracket with the threaded rod and wing nut—went into production on 6 May 1943 on Chevrolet serial #5-43-2005, Ordnance # 709, USA 6023542. **Above right:** A close-up of the cover for the crankcase oil filler for the left engine. (Reg Hodgson)

Top left: A shovel and tripod for a .30 caliber machine gun are stored on the side of the rear of the hull. **Top right**: The U-shaped steps are bent steel rods welded to the side of the rear of the lower hull. **Above left**: A towing pintle and mount are located at the center of the rear of the lower hull. **Above right**: Details of the towing pintle and exhausts. (Reg Hodgson)

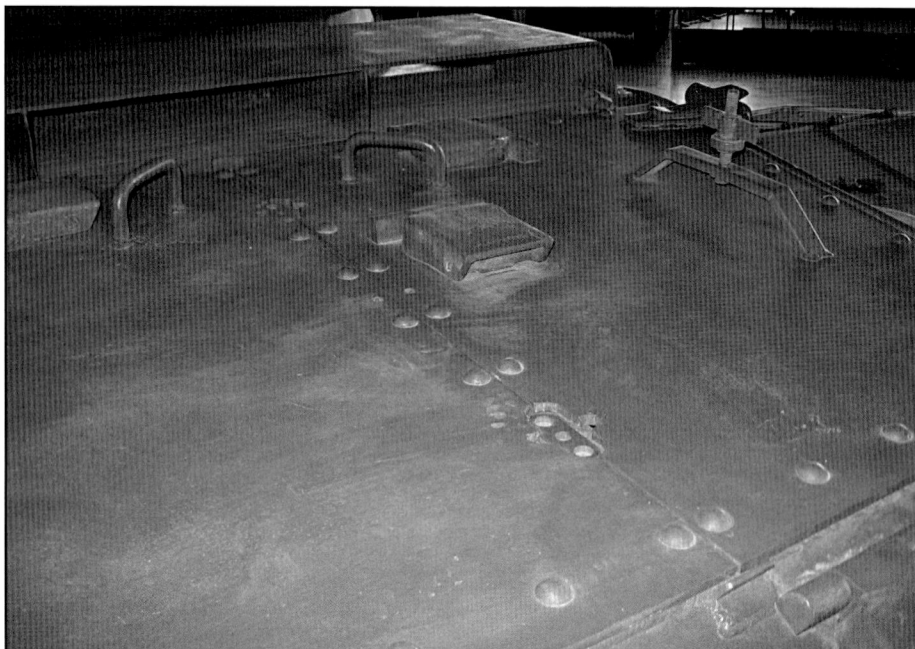

Top left: On this late production Staghound, protective guards have been welded to the hull near the bottoms of the mufflers. (Reg Hodgson) **Top right:** On this museum Staghound, date of acceptance late April 1943, the original bolted engine covers are modified to hinged, and the bolt holes are welded over. (Scott Taylor) **Above left:** The left side of the engine air intake shroud and grille, with a hinge visible to the lower left. (Scott Taylor) **Above right:** The engine covers, viewed from the right side of the Staghound. Note the axe stored on the side of the hull and the first aid kit container below it. (Reg Hodgson)

Left: The mufflers on this Staghound are a non-original longer type, extending well below the rear hull overhang. The retainer strap is not installed on the muffler in the foreground. **Right:** A view down into the tire chain box reveals two rows of holes in the bottom of the box to prevent water accumulation. Above the box is the cover for the filler tube of the main fuel tank. (Scott Taylor)

Top left: A close-up of a main fuel tank filler cap. Note the casting numbers on its surface. (Reg Hodgson) **Right:** A view up into the rear hull overhang. Note the support braces and electrical cables for the taillights. (Scott Taylor) **Above left:** A close-up of a towing pintle and its mounting. Note the U shaped bracket used to support the portable air compressor when installed. (Reg Hodgson)

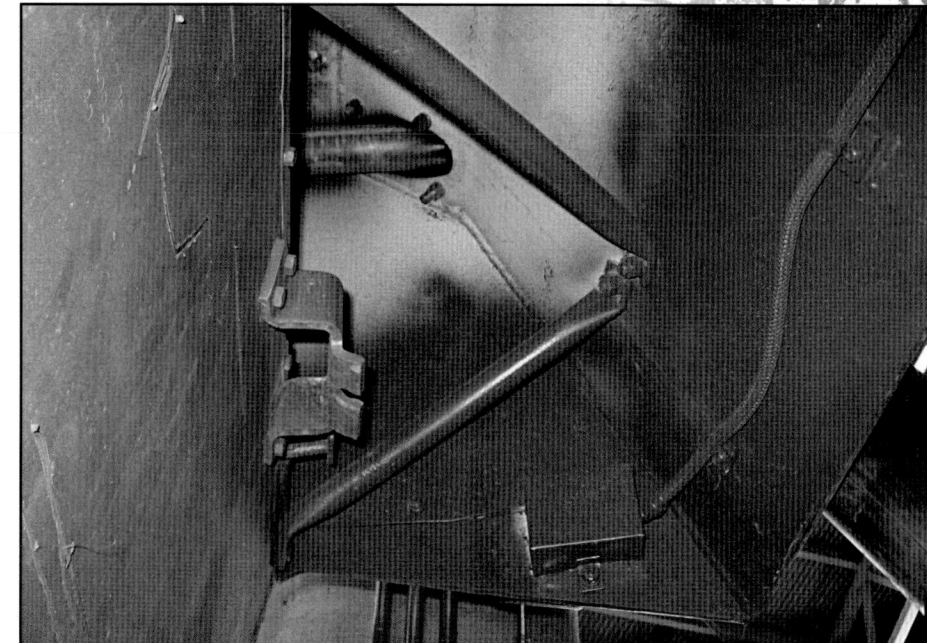

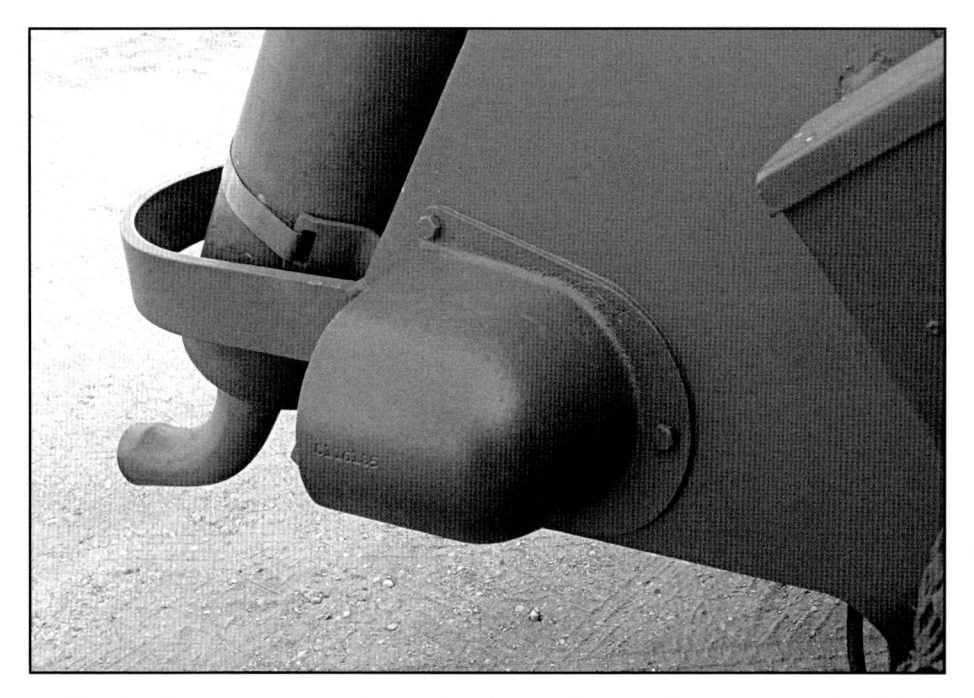

Top left: The right engine compartment fan is visible in this upward view into the rear hull overhang. The bottom of the tire chain box is to the upper left. (Scott Taylor) **Top right:** The right taillight junction box and cable is at the bottom center in this view of the right side of the rear hull overhang. (Scott Taylor) **Above left:** The scoop-shaped taillight guards are bolted onto the sides of the hull. To the left is a nonstandard U-shaped muffler guard. (Reg Hodgson) **Above right:** A roll of camouflage netting is strapped to the right rear fender. (Reg Hodgson)

Top left: A first aid kit is mounted on the rear of the hull over the right rear fender. (Reg Hodgson) **Top right, above left and right:** Later Staghounds had fold-down rear lifting eyes on the sides of the engine compartment. They were D-shaped and mounted with pins to brackets welded to the hull. Note the several cotter pins securing the eye to the pin and the lug on the center section, which acts as a stop. (Scott Taylor)

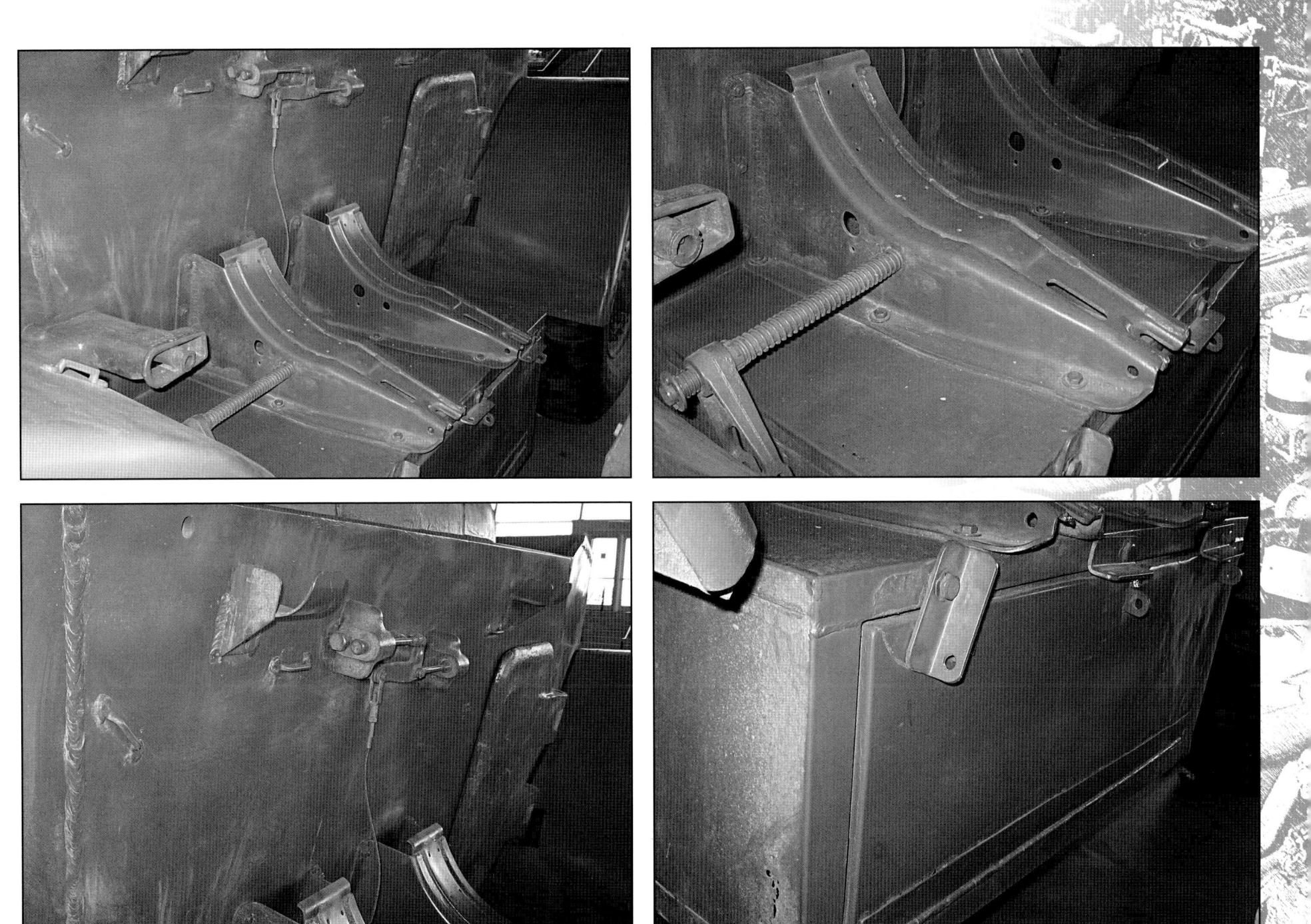

Top left: At the bottom of this photo are the support brackets for the right jettisonable fuel tank, with the release mechanism to the top and the housing for the valve at the lower left. **Top right:** The tanks could be released from the inside of the Staghound. The spring-loaded push-rod and fork at the left acted to release a quick-coupling with automatic shut-off valve. **Above left:** The brackets on either side of the release mechanism for the fuel tank held a fiber tube in which individual antenna sections were stored. **Above right:** The right storage box and lid. (Scott Taylor)

Left: Note the design of the hull door latch, including the operating lever and sliding latch pin. **Top right:** A liquid container is strapped to the rear of the front right fender. Note the weld seams of the armor plates. **Above right:** The bow machine gun provided extra firepower toward the front of the vehicle. This was a useful advantage when punching through lines of resistance; however, its angle of fire was very limited. (Reg Hodgson)

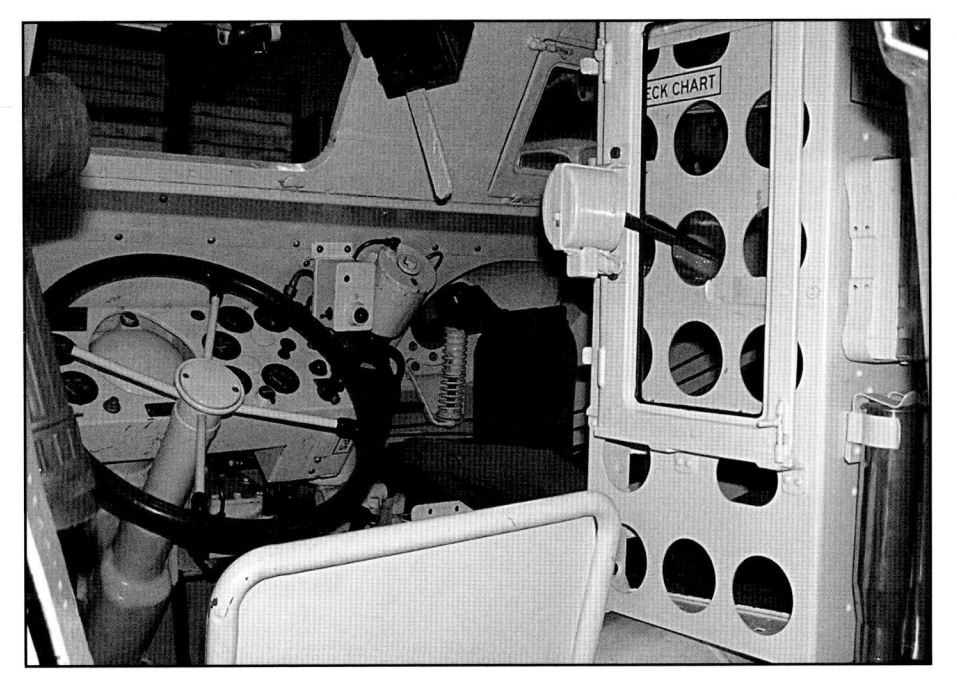

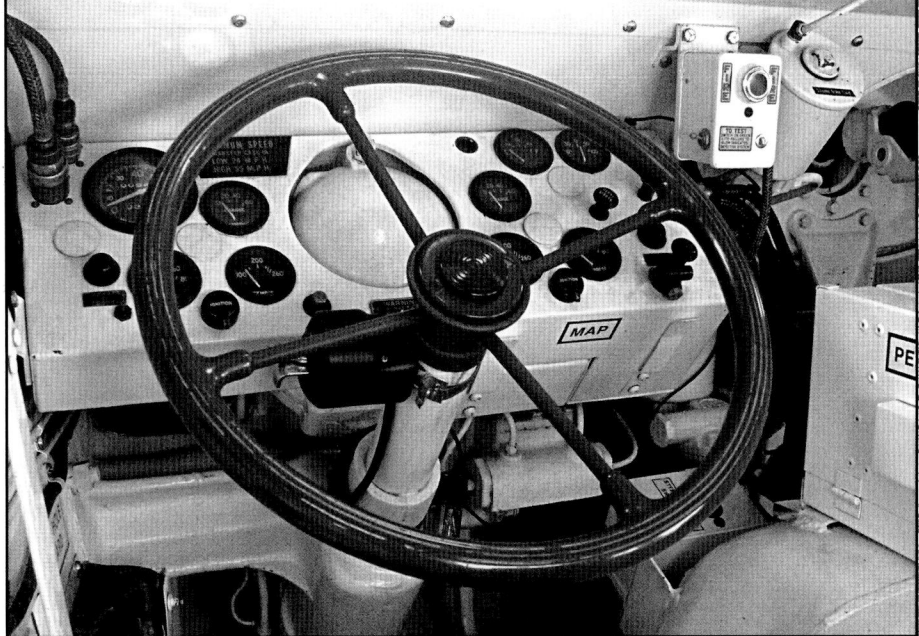

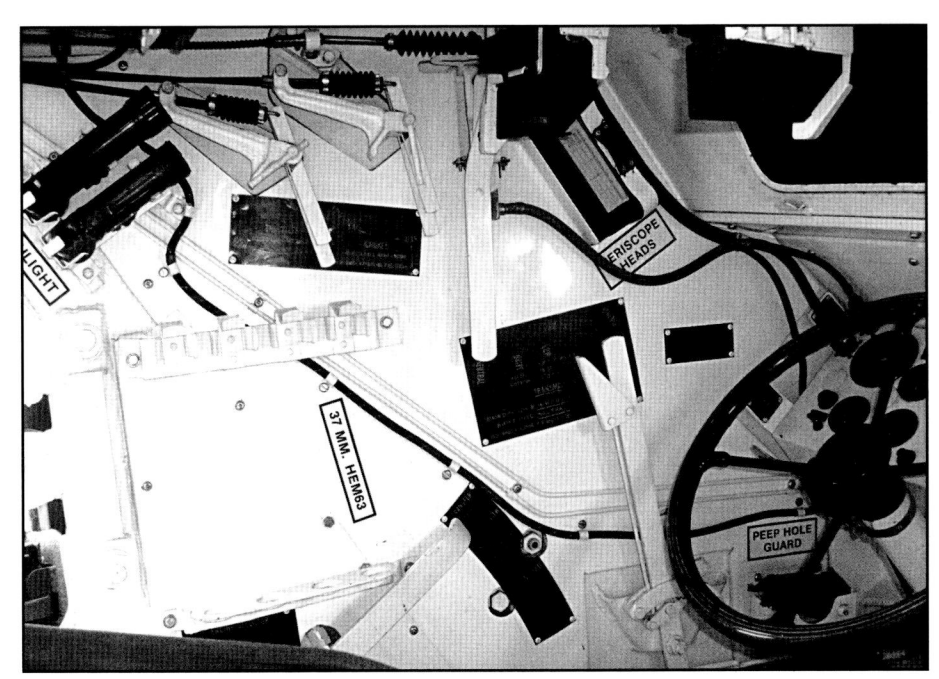

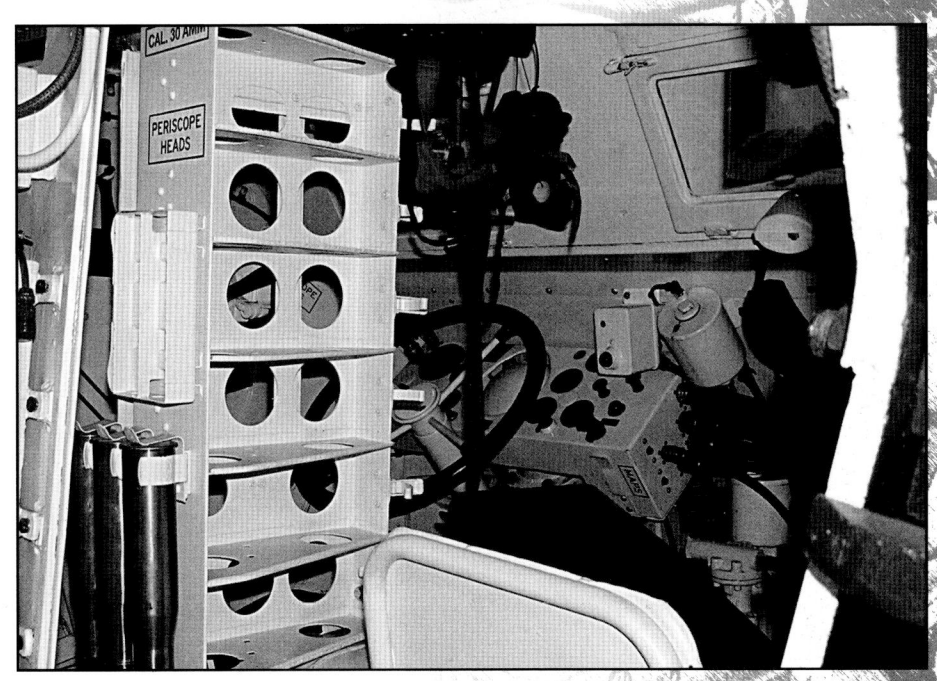

Top left: Between the driver's and the assistant driver's seats is a rack for storing .30 caliber ammunition boxes and periscope heads. (Marco Hogenkamp) **Top right:** The instrument panel is mounted in front of the steering wheel and includes gauges and switches for fuel and electrical systems, as well as both engines. (Reg Hodgson) **Above left:** On the hull wall to the driver's left are the choke and throttle levers (top left), transmission manual control lever (top center), and transfer case shift lever and hand brake (bottom). (Reg Hodgson) **Above right:** Storage clips for several 37mm rounds are on the rear of the ammunition rack. The assistant driver's seat is to the lower right. (Marco Hogenkamp)

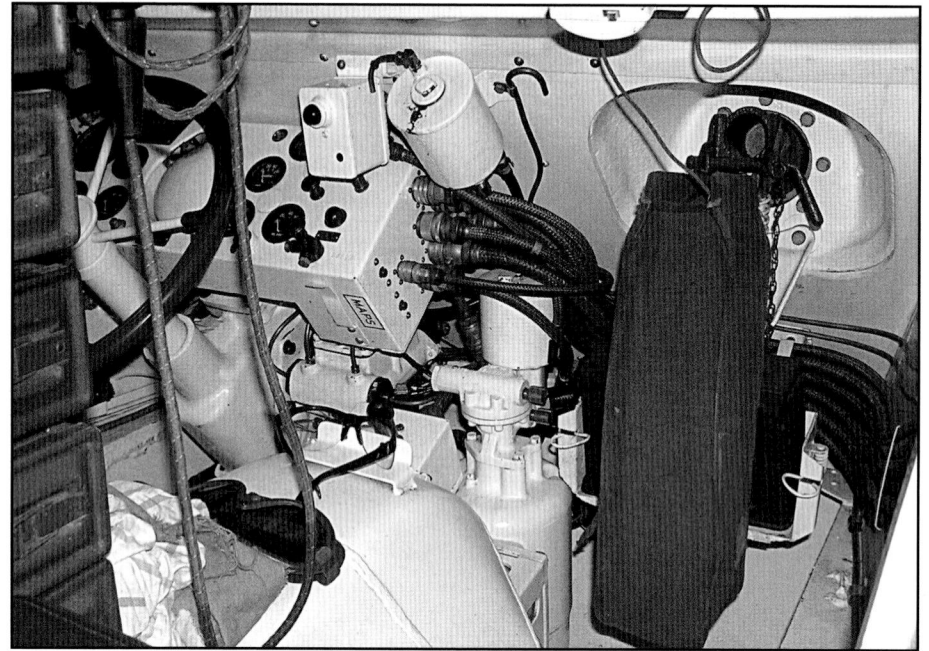

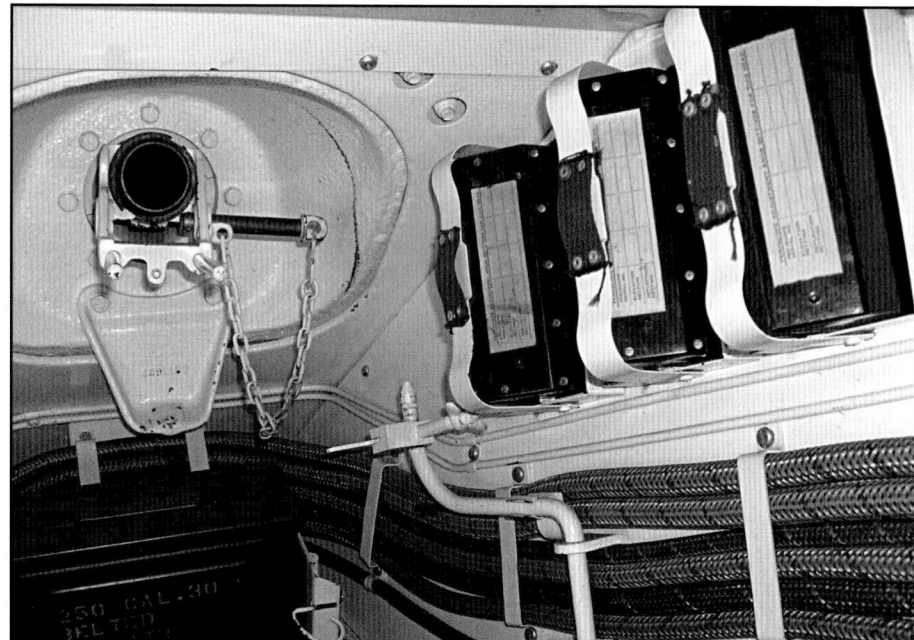

Left: A rack for storing .45 caliber ammunition clips for a Thompson submachine gun are to the right of the assistant driver's seat. His open viewing door is to the upper right, with the mount for the bow machine gun below it. To the top right is his stored windshield. (Reg Hodgson) **Top right:** A spent-brass collector bag is attached to the bow machine gun mount in this Staghound. At the lower center of the photo is a large 24-volt electrical motor which drives the hydraulic steering pump mounted on top of it and the reservoir for the power-steering system. The cylinder at the top center is the hydraulic oil reservoir for the brakes and the hydraulic throttle. (Marco Hogenkamp) **Above right:** Above the neatly arranged braided electrical cables are periscope heads. The bow machine gun mount is to the left. (Reg Hodgson)

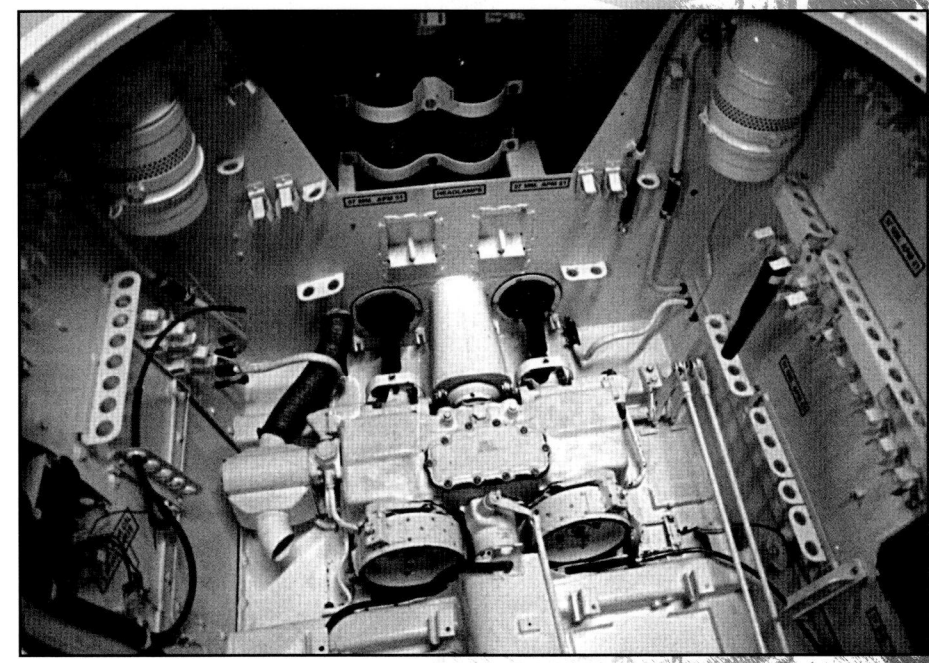

Top left: The assistant driver's detachable windshield is stowed above and to the right of his seat; note the windshield wiper and motor. (Reg Hodgson) **Top right:** A Thompson submachine gun is stored to the rear of the rack for ammunition clips. (Reg Hodgson) **Above left:** The open right door as viewed through the assistant driver's forward vision door, with the turret basket to the left. (Reg Hodgson) **Above right:** At the rear of the crew compartment are the oil bath air cleaners (top right and left) and numerous clips for 37mm ammunition. The two fixed fire extinguishers are visible at the top center; at the bottom is the transfer case. Note the round tunnels for the drive shafts, a late-production feature; earlier Staghounds had square tunnels. (Marco Hogenkamp)

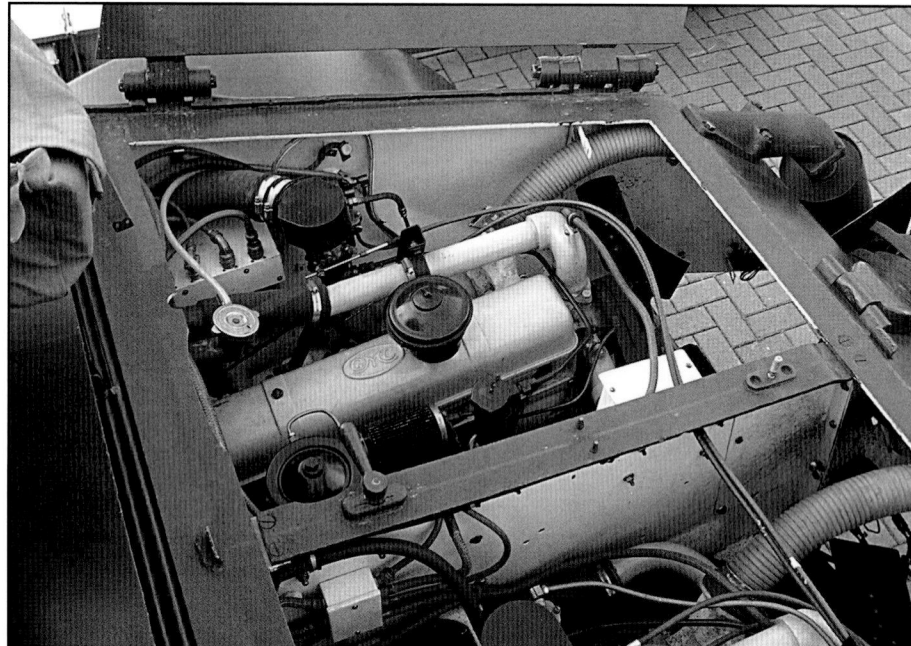

Top and above left: The left engine compartment holds one of two GMC 270 CID engines, seen at different angles in these two photos. The Staghound's engines were developed specifically for that vehicle, although they shared a few interchangeable parts with the CCKW 352 and 353. **Top and above right:** These two views show a Staghound's right engine and engine compartment. Note the bulkhead that separates the two engine compartments. (Marco Hogenkamp)

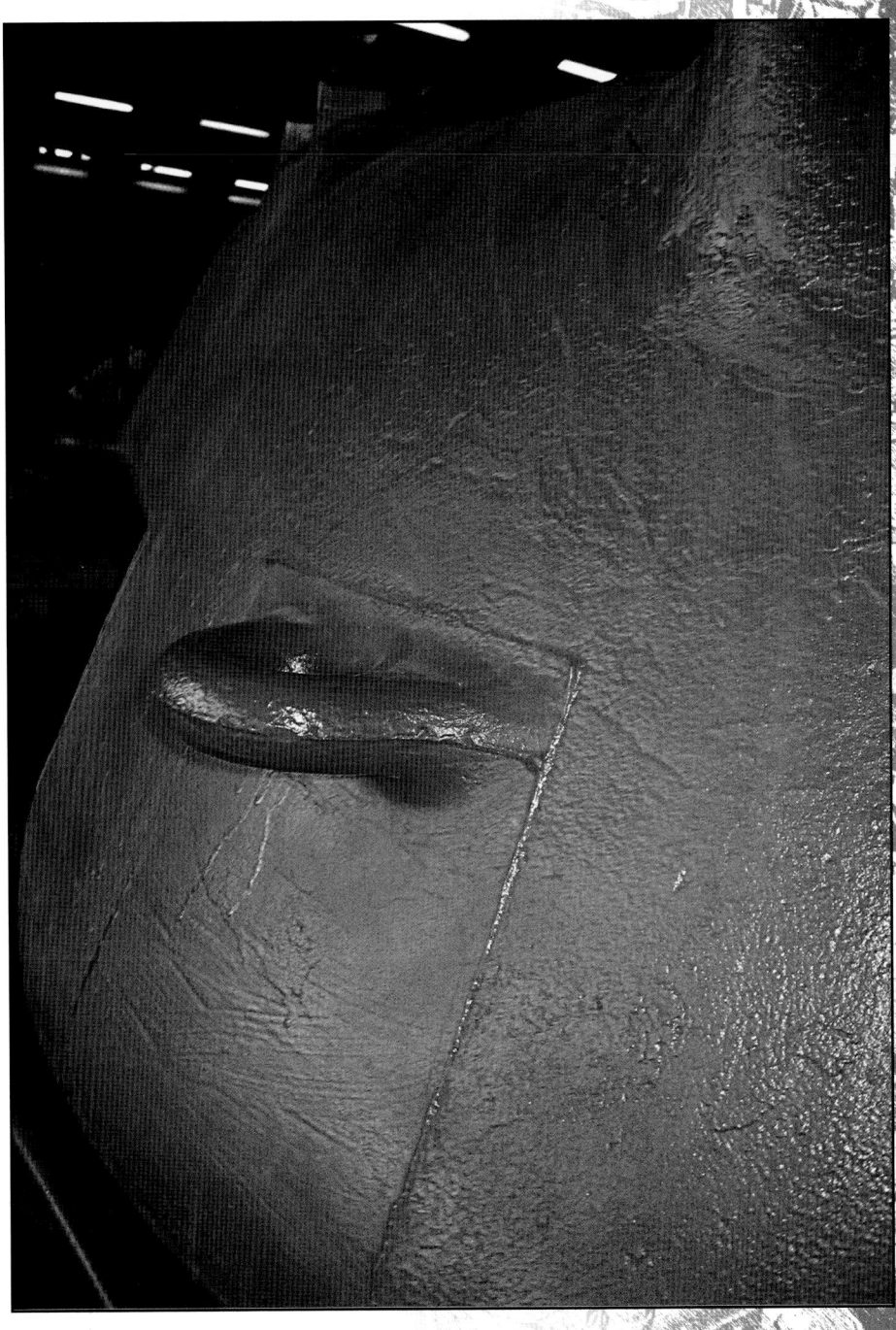

Top left: The gun shield of the M24A1 gun mount of later T17E1 Staghounds is identifiable by its angular lines and the manner in which it projects from the front of the mount. (Reg Hodgson) **Above left:** Below the M24A1 gun mount's shield is a shot deflector, intended to prevent projectiles from striking the vulnerable area beneath the gun shield when the 37mm gun was elevated. (Scott Taylor) **Right:** Note the seams on and adjacent to the lifting eye on the side of the turret. (Scott Taylor)

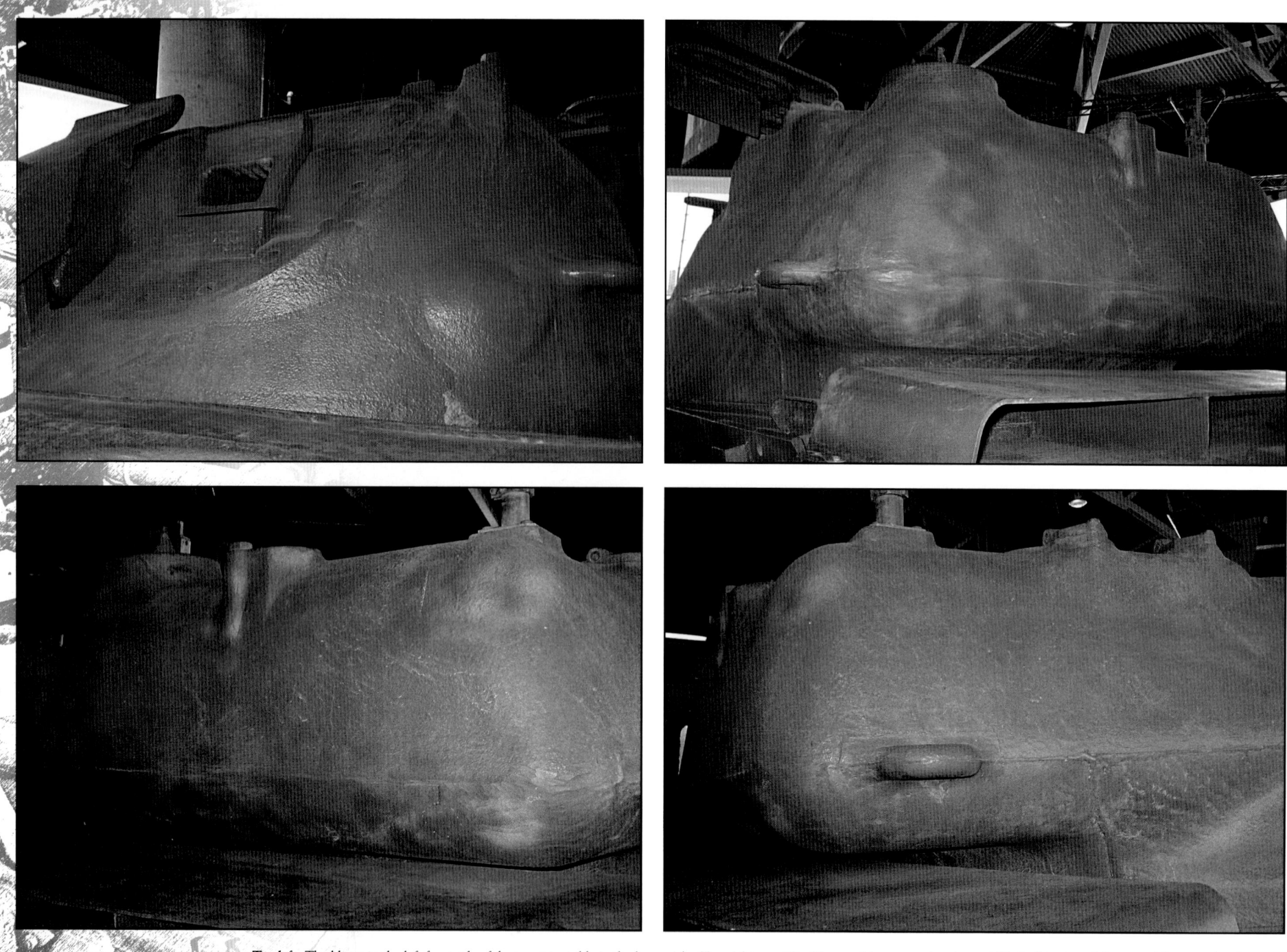

Top left: The blister in the left front side of the turret is visible to the lower right. **Top right:** The left side of the turret bustle has various casting seams. The engine air intake shroud is to the bottom. **Above left:** The various protrusions for antenna mounts and (at center) the .30 caliber machine gun pedestal are visible in this view of the rear of the turret bustle. **Above right:** The right rear of the turret of this late Staghound includes an integral lifting eye. (Scott Taylor)

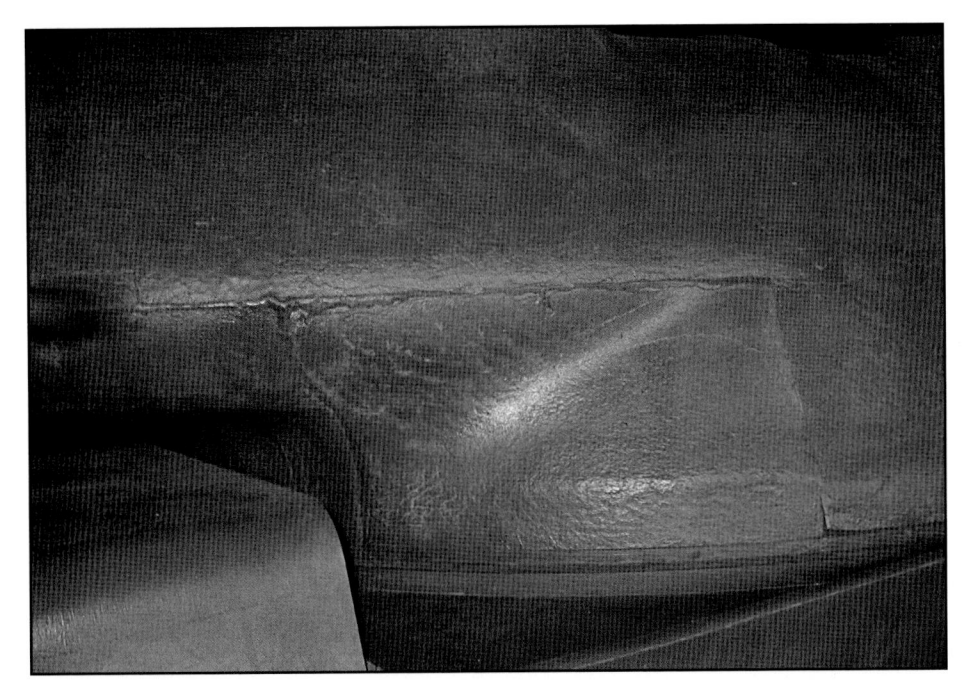

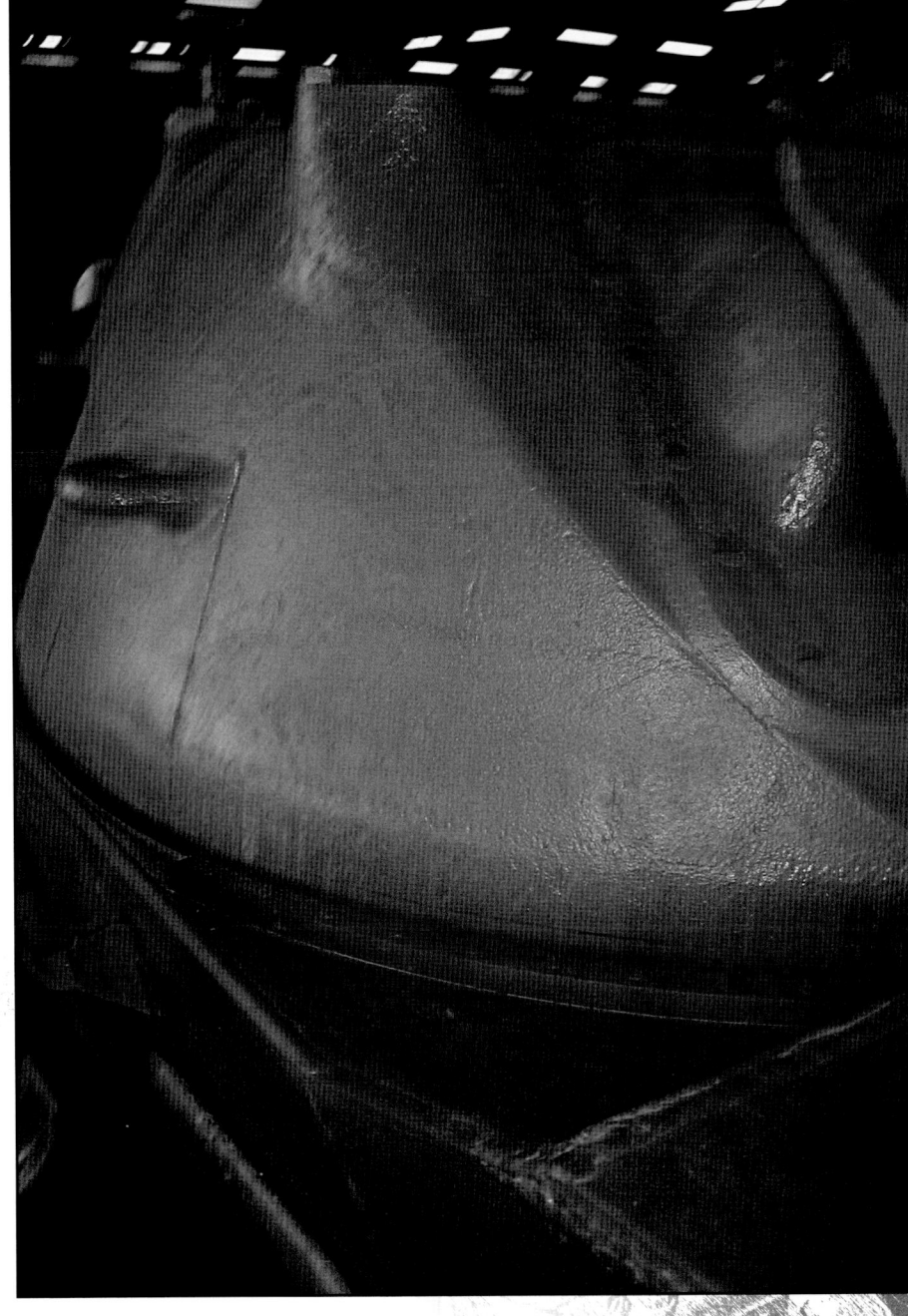

Top left: Note the details of the seams at the lower right rear of the turret. (Scott Taylor)
Right: The lifting eye at the front right side of a late Staghound, with part of the M24A1 gun mount to the right. (Scott Taylor) **Above left:** In this view of the turret roof of a late Staghound, the spotlight is at the center and is flanked by periscopes. Note the small vane sight in front of the gunner's periscope; this was a factory installation. (Reg Hodgson)

Top left: The pedestal at the rear of this Staghound turret holds an M1919A4 .30 caliber machine gun on a cradle mount. (Reg Hodgson) **Above left:** Camouflage netting has been draped over the turret of a Staghound. A roll of this netting was standard issue. (Marco Hogenkamp) **Right:** A wooden ammunition box is attached to the left side of the cradle. In the foreground is the base of a wireless antenna. (Reg Hodgson)

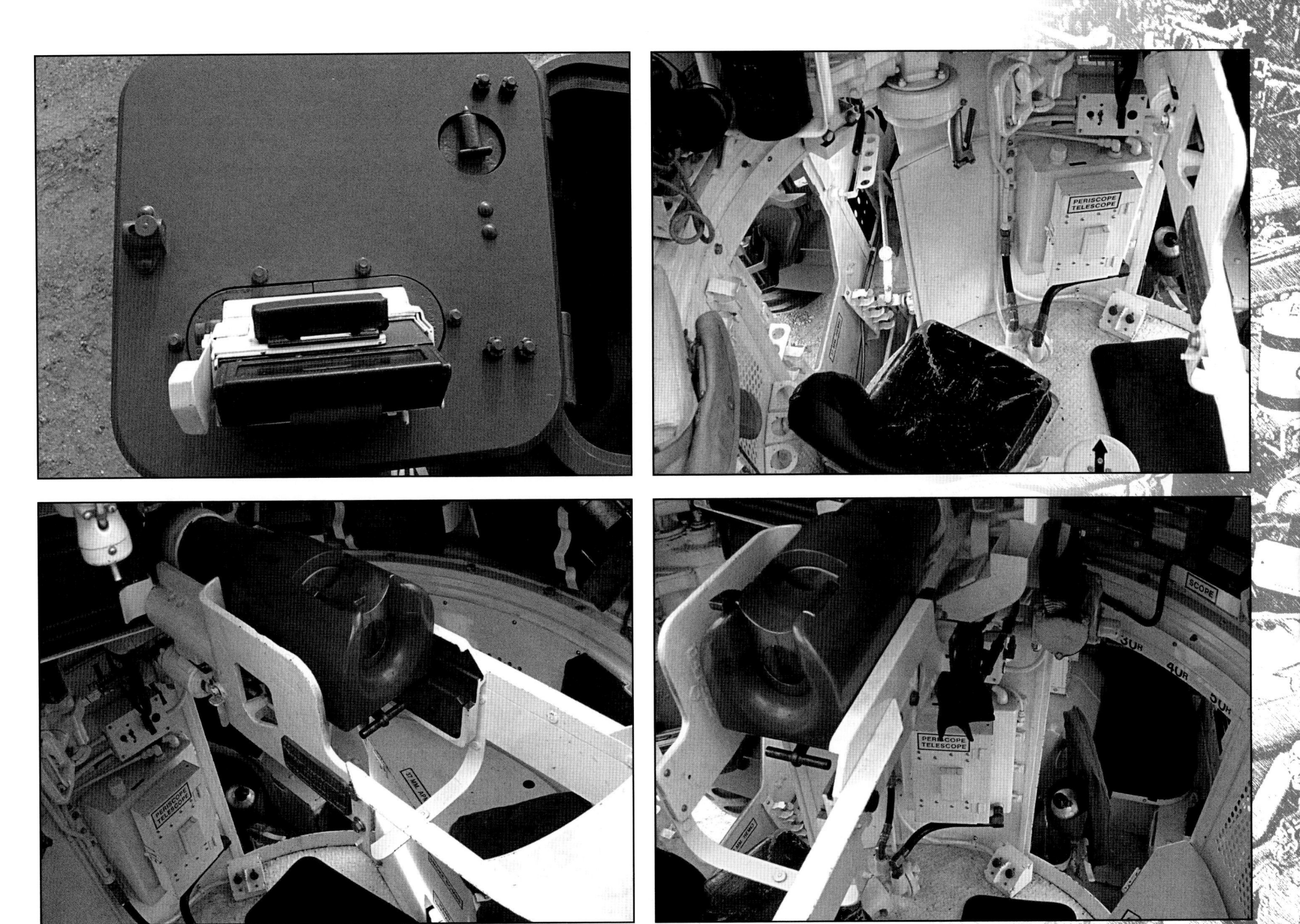

Top left: The rear part of the commander's hatch has a non-revolving periscope. On the left of the hatch is a latch. **Top right:** The gunner's seat, traversing controls, and the 37mm gun's recoil shield are visible through the commander's hatch. **Above left:** The breech of the M6 37mm gun is at the top center. Note the data plate on the side of the recoil guard.

Above right: In the loader's area of the turret, the black numbers visible at the top of the opening in the turret basket are azimuth references in 10-degree increments. These helped to roughly determine the orientation of the turret and main gun. (Reg Hodgson)

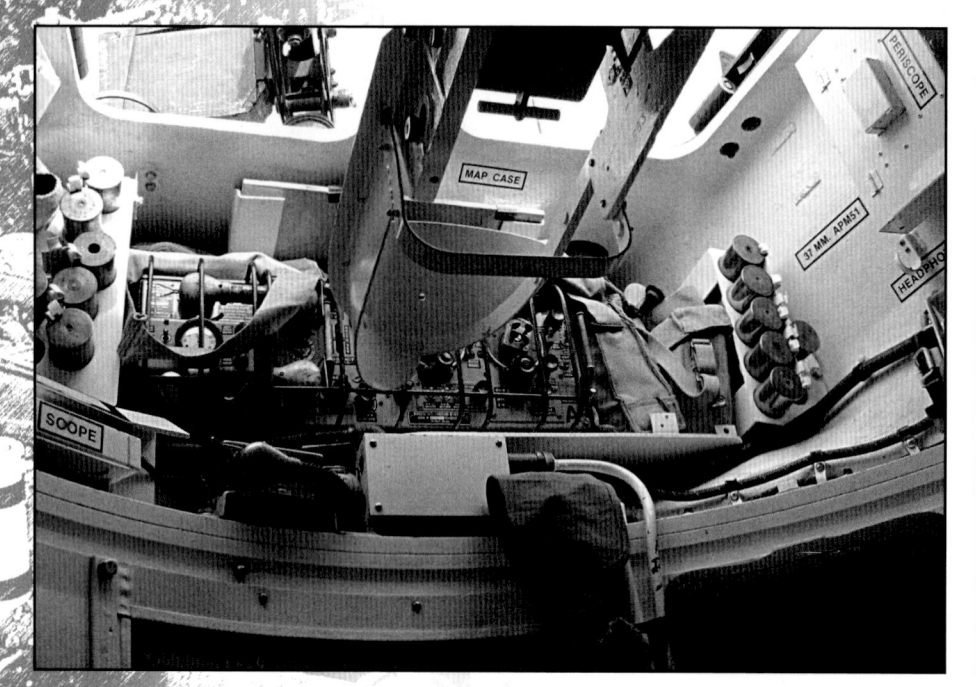

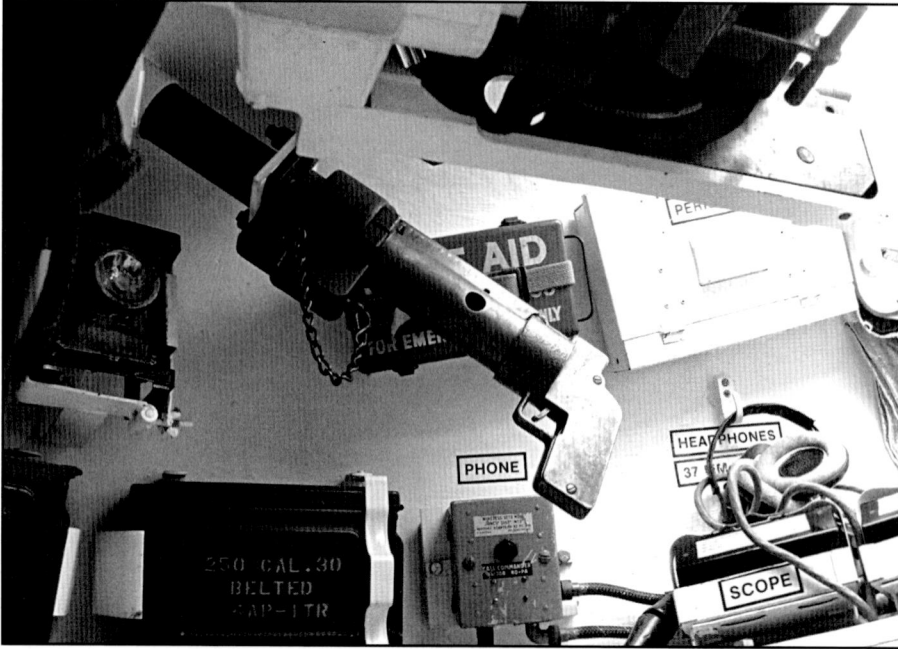

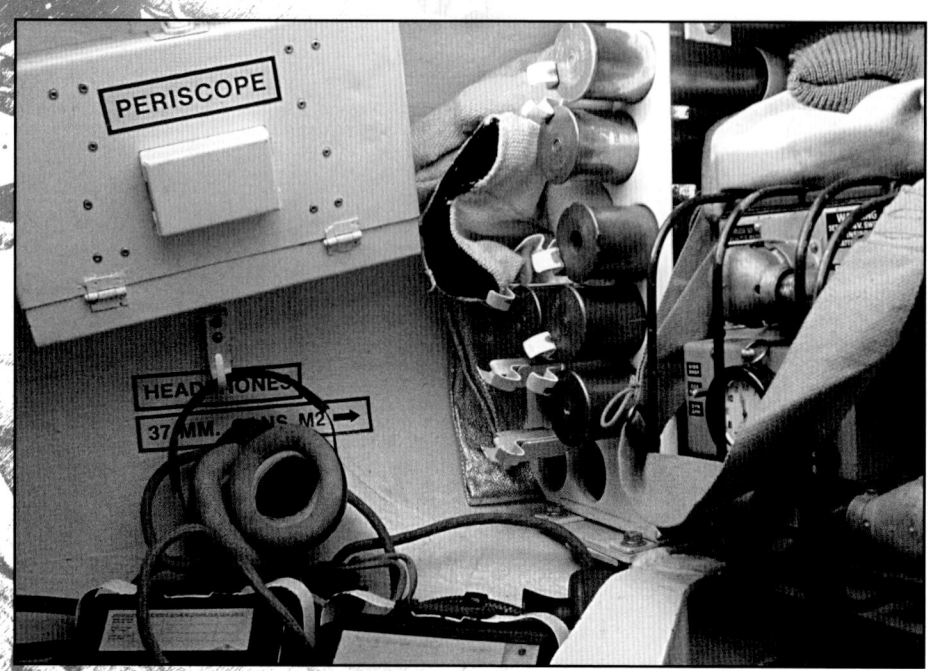

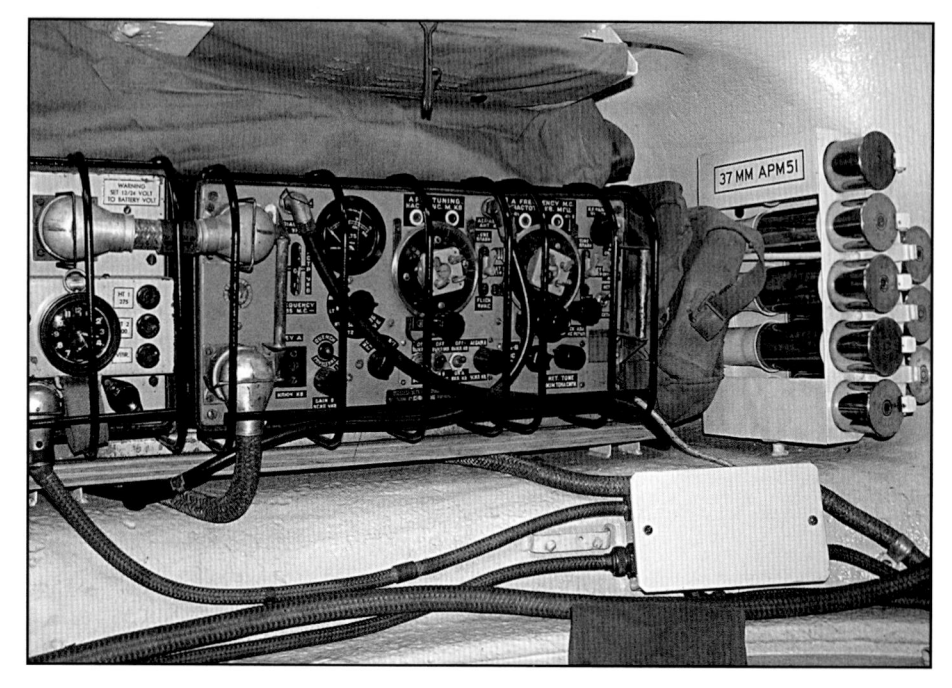

Top left: As viewed from the floor of the turret basket looking upward and toward the rear, the No. 19 wireless set is in the turret bustle. (Reg Hodgson) **Top right:** Looking from below the 37mm gun toward the right side of the turret is a Bombthrower M3 or Mk I (A), along with an intercom box, stowage for .30 caliber ammunition, periscope heads and other items. On the left is a British Hellesen lamp, a type of emergency light. (Reg Hodgson) **Above left and right**: In the rear corners of the turret on both sides of the wireless set are racks for 37mm canister rounds. (Marco Hogenkamp)

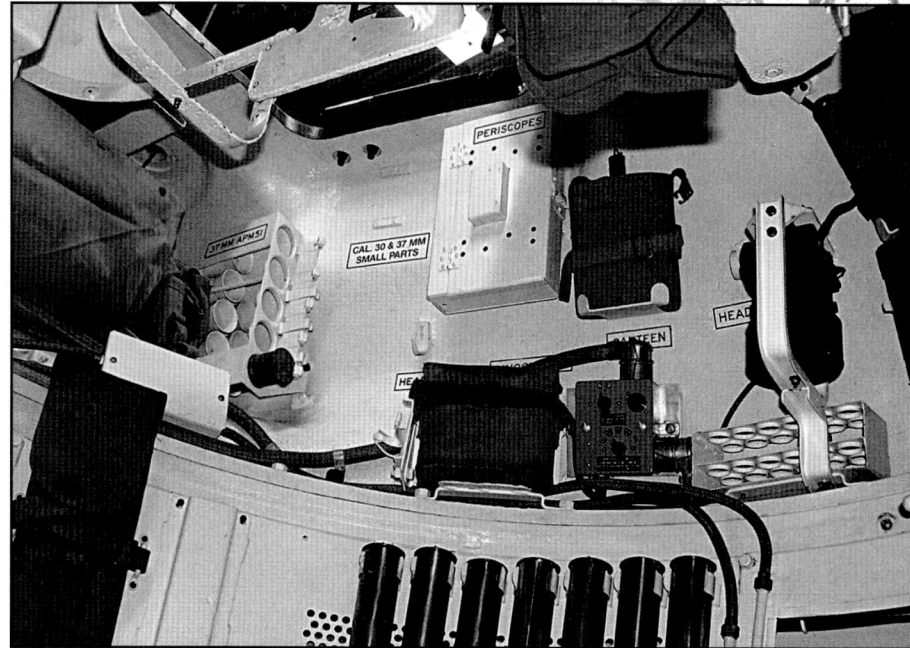

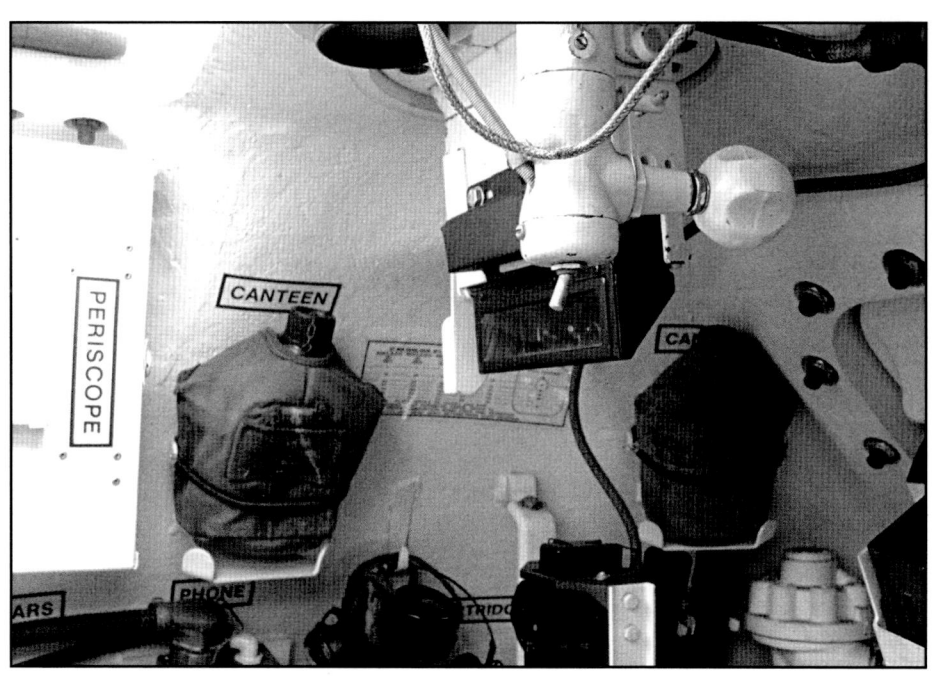

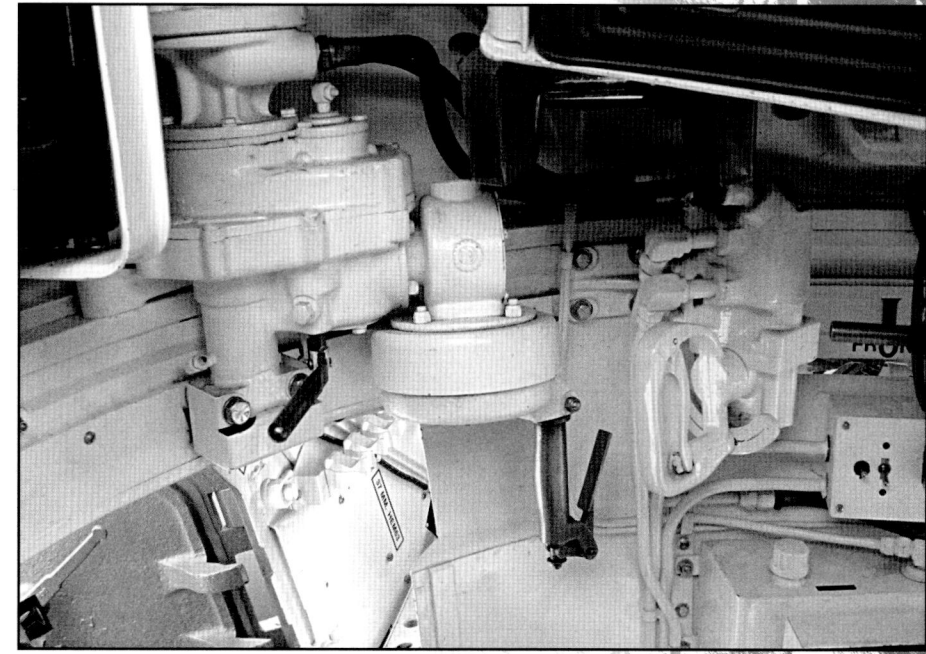

Top left: The two fixed fire extinguisher bottles are in a recess behind the rear bulkhead of the crew compartment; two headlight assemblies are stashed beside them. (Reg Hodgson)
Top right: Items stored on the left side of the turret include British-type canteens, binoculars, spare periscope, compass and flashlight. (Marco Hogenkamp) **Above left:** In a different Staghound, American canteens are stored to the front of the periscope box. On the near side of the gunner's periscope is the operating handle of the spotlight on the turret roof. (Reg Hodgson) **Above right:** To the front of the gunner's position are the hydraulic traversing motor gearbox (left), manual traversing hand wheel (center) and hydraulic traverse controls (right). The dark colored lever below the traversing motor shifts the traverse operation between manual and powered. (Reg Hodgson)

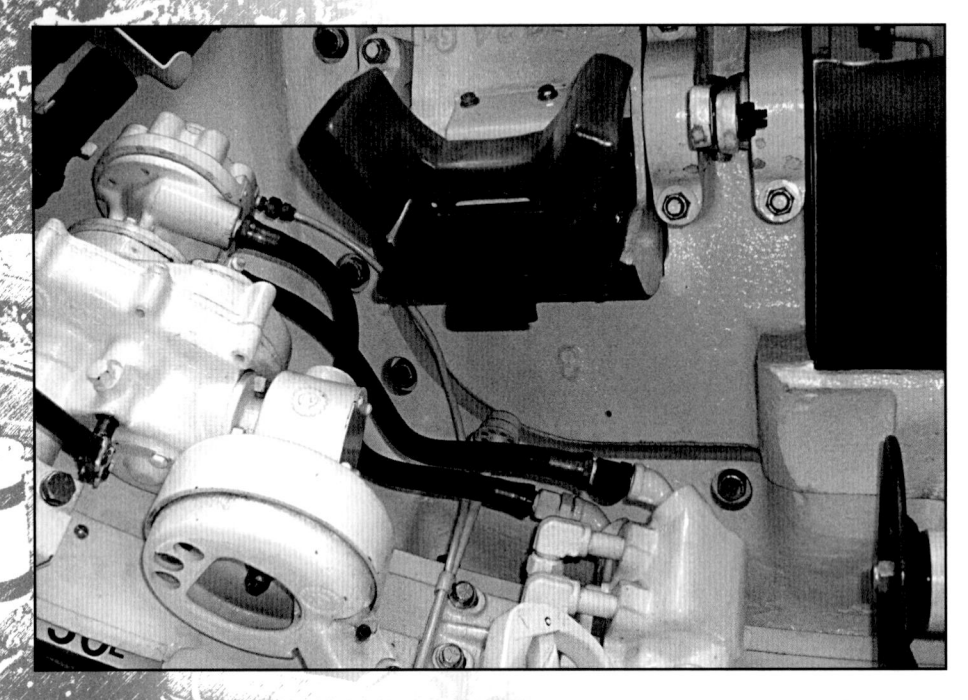

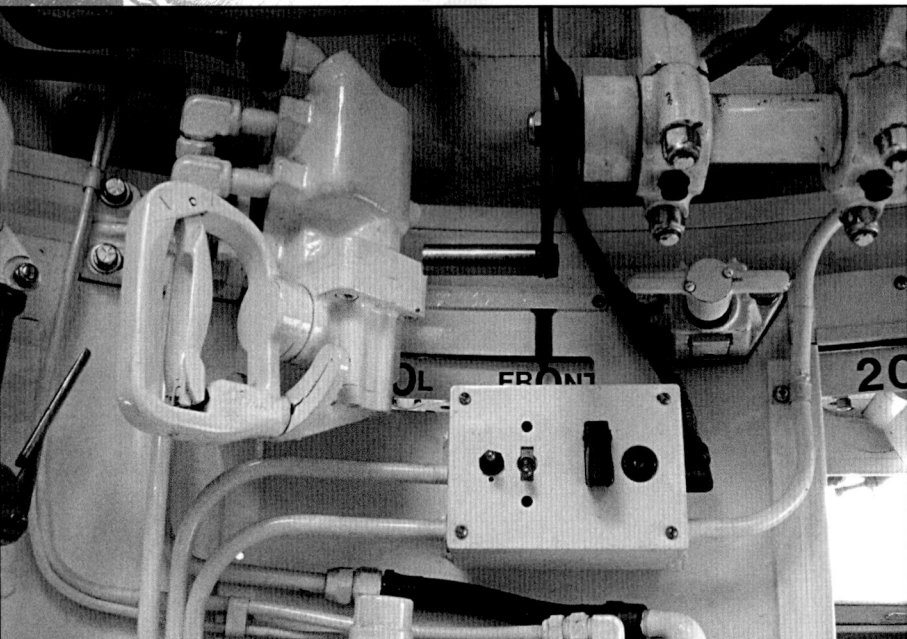

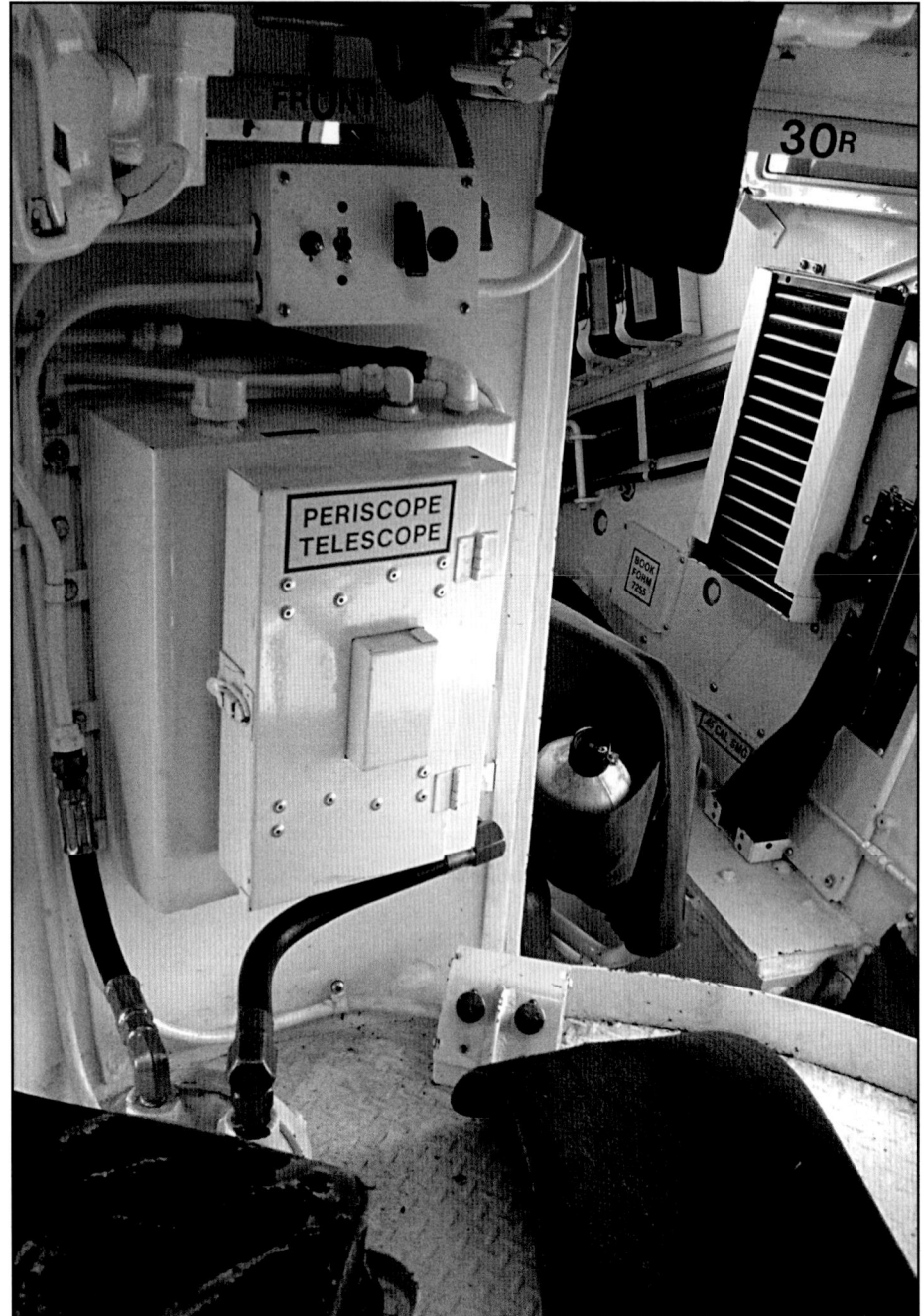

Top left: In this view from below, the gunner's periscope is at the top center with the hydraulic traversing motor and manual traversing handwheel below it. **Above left:** The powered traverse of the turret was actuated by turning the handle at left either right or left. To the lower right of the control handle are the turret power, dome lamp and firing safety switches. At the top right is the elevating hand wheel. (Reg Hodgson) **Right:** At the front of the turret basket, the box to which the gunner's periscope/telescope box is attached is the hydraulic oil reservoir. The assistant driver's area is visible through the opening in the turret basket.

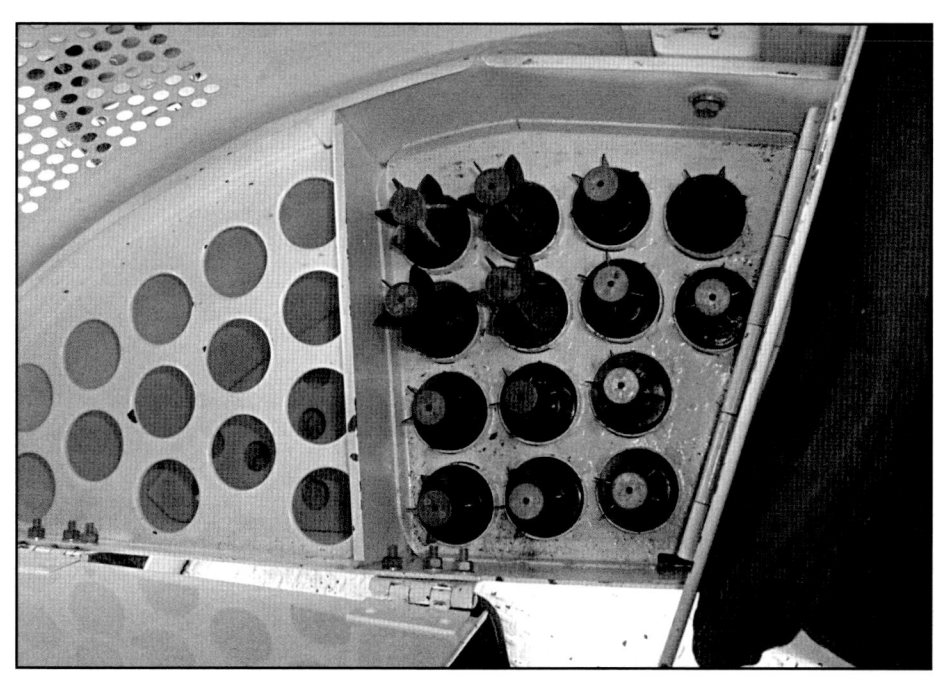

Top left: The loader/wireless operator's seat is on top of a bin holding 37mm ammunition, smoke bombs and grenades. (Reg Hodgson) **Top right:** In the forward section of the bin is storage for 37mm rounds. (Marco Hogenkamp) **Above left:** A rack holding 14 smoke bombs—note the stabilizing fins—is to the rear of the 37mm ammunition rack. (Reg Hodgson) **Above right:** On the floor of the turret basket are the vehicle directional indicator (left), and the hydraulic motor and pump (right). In the background are racks for 37mm ammunition. (Marco Hogenkamp)

T17E2

Developed in early 1943, the T17E2 armored car was a T17E1 Staghound hull with a Frazer-Nash twin .50 caliber machine gun turret in place of the 37mm gun turret. The electro-hydraulically powered turret had a traverse rate of up to 60 degrees per second. The vehicle in this photo is a late production example whose turret has rounded sides; earlier vehicles had a turret fabricated from flat, welded plates. (The Patton Museum via Don Moriarty)

Top left: The pilot T17E2 was photographed on 20 March 1943 at Aberdeen Proving Ground. Note its flat-sided turret and the absence of a storage box and jettisonable fuel tank on the hull side. (The Patton Museum via Don Moriarty) **Right:** T17E2s move down an assembly line. To the left are three turret baskets awaiting installation. Notice that the lead vehicle has periscope cages fitted to all three periscope positions, an unusual configuration. (Military History Institute via Jim Gilmore) **Above left:** This early T17E2 has the jettisonable fuel tanks and storage boxes installed. Note the two antennae at the front of the hull. (The Patton Museum via Don Moriarty)

Left: A turret basket is lowered into the hull of a T17E2. The basket would hold one crewman: the gunner. (Military History Institute via Jim Gilmore) **Top right:** This T17E2 had the late-model, rounded turret sides and early-type headlight mounts. (The Patton Museum via Don Moriarty) **Above right:** The T17E2's .50 caliber machine guns had an elevation of -10 degrees to +80 degrees, and a 360-degree traverse. It used a Navy Mk IX gunsight and could carry 2,610 rounds of .50 caliber ammunition. (The Patton Museum via Don Moriarty)

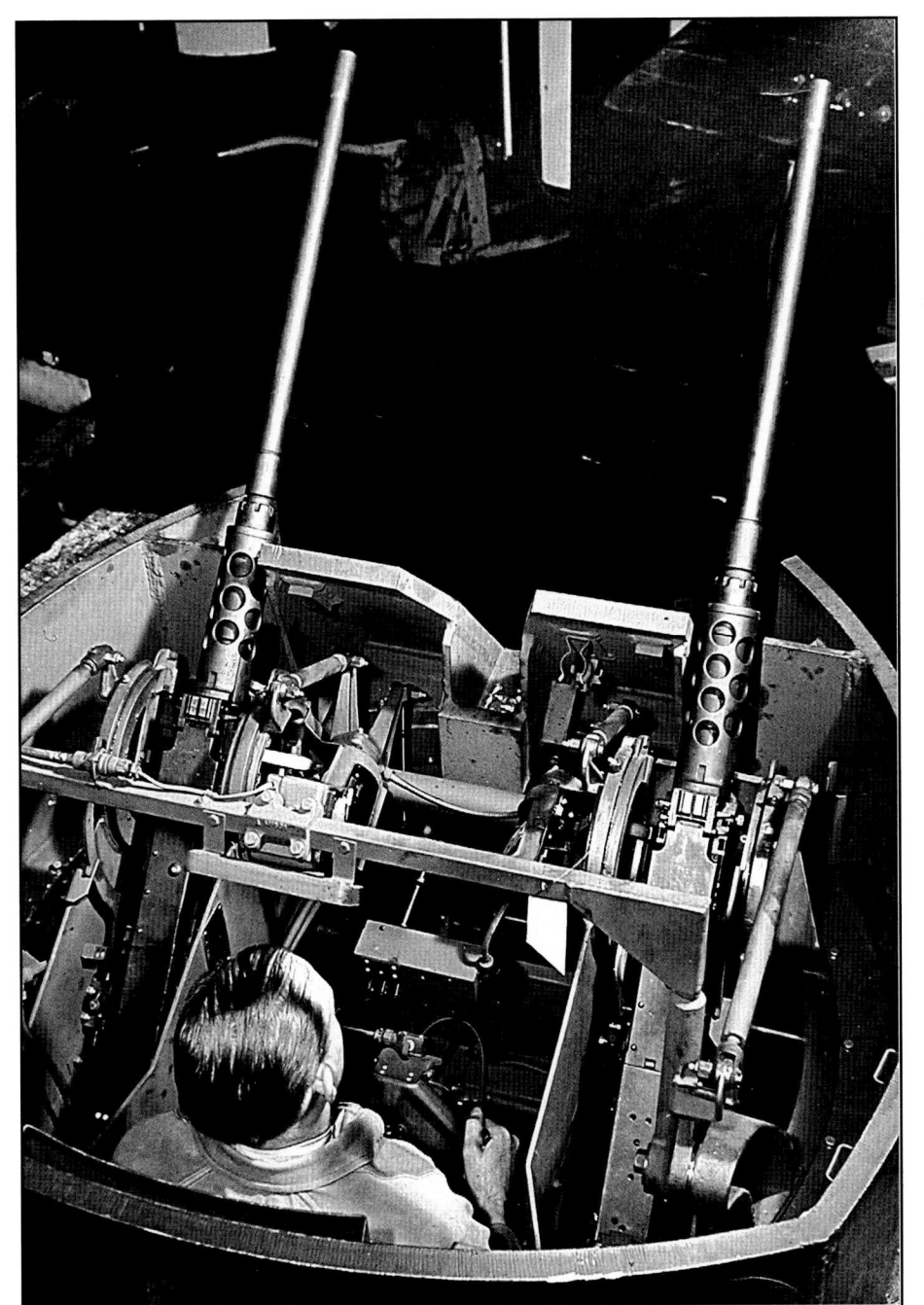

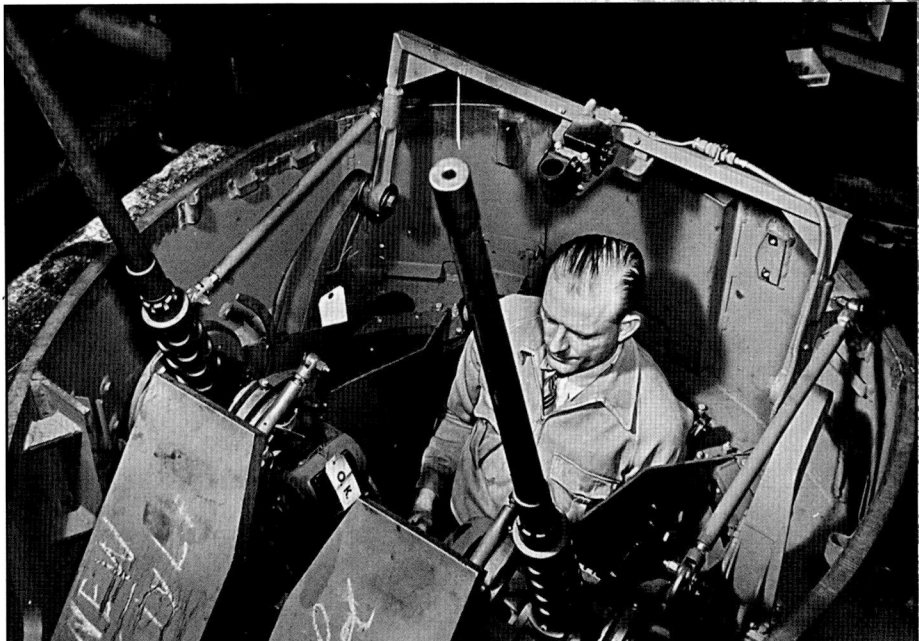

Left: The turret of the T17E2 was protected by armor 1.25 inches thick. The plate between the guns was set at a 45-degree angle, multiplying the effective protection. The gunner had a handlebar-type elevation and traverse control. (Military History Institute via Jim Gilmore)

Top right: The Mk IX gunsight is above the test gunner's head and rests on a crossbar mechanically linked to the machine gun cradles. (Military History Institute via Jim Gilmore)

Above right: This T17E2 is in the field with a tarp over the turret. (Marco Hogenkamp)

The late-model T17E1 hull of this T17E2 is visible in this overhead view. Note the raised side armor of the hull next to the turret, the hinged engine covers and their sand channel brackets. The bow machine gun and its mounting bulge were completely eliminated to make room for the relocated No. 19 wireless set. (The Tank Museum, Bovington, Dorset)

Top left: The bow of a surviving T17E2 stored at the Military Vehicle Technology Foundation exhibits the clean glacis without a bow machine gun bulge characteristic of this variant. **Top right:** The T17E2 turret is situated on a base that fits over the larger opening it requires. The A-antenna mount for the WS-19 wireless set is visible on the left side of the previous photo. **Above left:** Although the late T17E2 had a rounded turret, it was fabricated from several plates in such a manner that it did not have a circular plan. The tie-down hooks can secure a cover over the open top of the turret. **Above right:** An overhead view of the T17E2 engine deck, looking from the turret to the rear. Note that the engine covers are of the late type.

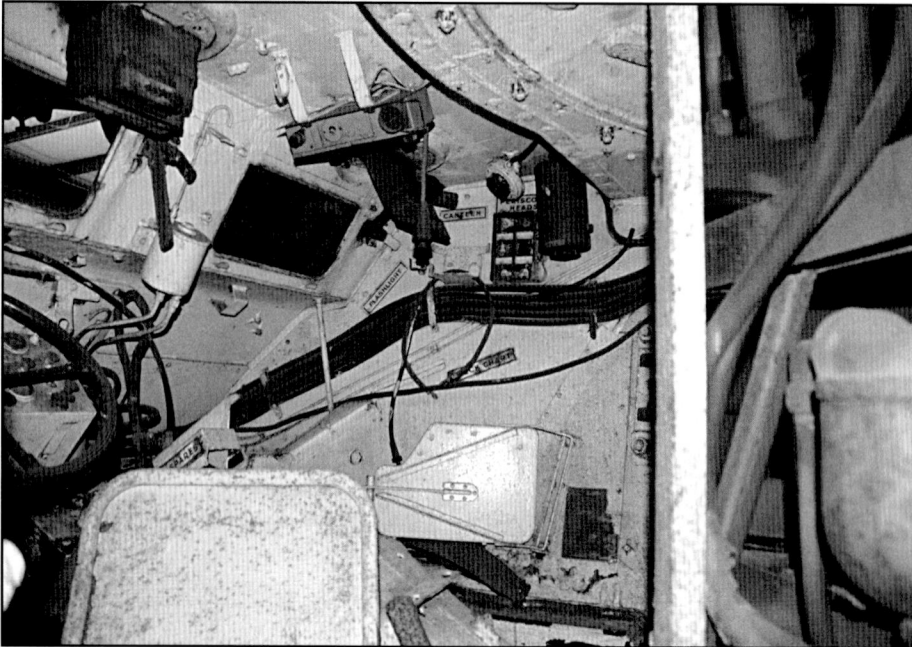

Top left: This T17E2 has U-shaped muffler guards added to its rear plate. **Top right:** In a view facing toward the right front of the crew compartment, the driver's seat is to the left and the turret basket is to the right. Note the bracket on the lower rear armor plate for installing a pintle hook. **Above left:** This T17E2 has the late, 37-gallon jettisonable fuel tanks. (The Patton Museum via Don Moriarty) **Above right:** The design and manner of installation of the canvas cover for the T17E2 turret is visible here. Note the lashings securing the bottom of the cover to the tie-down hooks. (The Patton Museum via Don Moriarty)

T17E3

In November 1943 the British issued a requirement for 100 armored cars fitted with the M8 howitzer motor carriage's turret and 75mm howitzer. Chevrolet produced and tested a prototype, the T17E3, based on the hull of a late T17E1, registration number USA 6024950. This is the same vehicle shown in its original configuration on pages 50 and 51. Chevrolet ceased development of the T17E3 when the British rescinded their requirement. The vehicle is shown without the air inlet cover in place. (The Patton Museum via Don Moriarty)

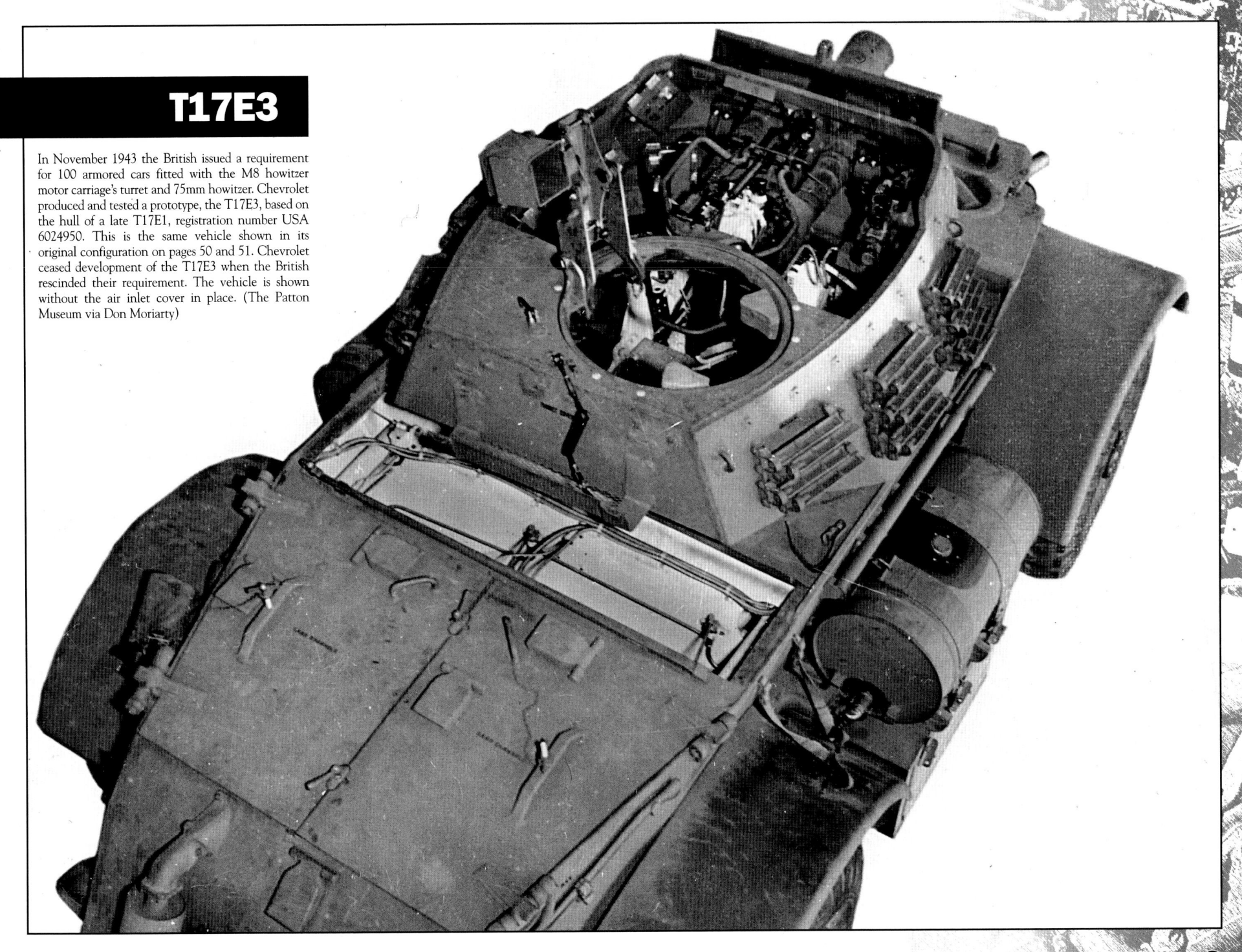

The turret of the T17E3 prototype had a manual traverse of 360 degrees and armor one inch thick on the sides and 1.5 inches thick on the front and the howitzer shield. The 75mm howitzer had an elevation of -20 to +40 degrees. Protruding above the top of the turret is the mount for an M2 .50 caliber antiaircraft machine gun, positioned on the ring mount at the right rear of the turret. (The Patton Museum via Don Moriarty)

Staghound II

Mixed in with a row of Polish Staghound Is are two Staghound IIs, which are basically Staghound Is outfitted with 3" tank howitzers in lieu of the 37mm gun. Other modifications incorporated into the Staghound II were the elimination of the bow machine gun and the substitution of external, 4-inch smoke dischargers for the 2-inch smoke mortar mounted inside the turret. The 4-inch smoke dischargers are visible on the side of the second vehicle's turret. (The Tank Museum, Bovington, Dorset)

On 28 June 1945, this Staghound II of the Royal Canadian Dragoons participated in the victory parade in Amsterdam, Holland. The vehicle has clean configuration with extra stowed gear removed, including the smoke grenade launchers from the mounting on the side of the turret next to the commander. Because the commander's hatch on the Staghound Mk II was configured with hinges on the forward side, a tall hatch rest was added to the front of the turret roof so the hatch did not lie on the adjacent periscope when open. (Clive M. Law, Service Publications)

Staghound III

The British took advantage of a surplus of Crusader Mk III tank turrets left over from the conversion of Crusader chassis to special-purpose vehicles by mounting the turrets on a number of T17E1 hulls. These vehicles were designated Staghound IIIs. The Staghound III's turret basket was adapted to fit under the turret. The turret's armament consisted of an Ordnance QF 75mm main gun and coaxial 7.92mm Besa machine gun. The jettisonable fuel tanks were eliminated and replaced by extra storage boxes of various designs. (The Patton Museum via Don Moriarty)

The housings for the jettisonable fuel tank's valve were not eliminated from the Staghound III. They are visible to the rear of the side storage box, below the methyl-bromide fire extinguisher. This vehicle has the early-type fixed lifting eye over the rear fender. (The Patton Museum via Don Moriarty)

The assistant driver's position was eliminated in the Staghound III to make room for more 75mm ammunition storage space. Consequently, the bow machine gun was deleted and the opening covered by a conical armor plug. Interior modifications to the stock Crusader III turret included the addition of a commander's seat and British-type hydraulic traverse controls. This vehicle has early-type headlight mounts. (The Patton Museum via Don Moriarty)

This Staghound III lacks the X-shaped stiffeners on the door of the upper storage box that were present on the vehicle shown on page 120. In addition, the side profile of the coaming of this vehicle's loader's hatch is of a different, non-rectangular shape. It also differs in other details. Note the tripod-type rearview mirror supports on the front fenders. (The Tank Museum, Bovington, Dorset)

The top two-thirds of the stowage bin added to the Staghound III have a beveled or tilted profile and include an access door. The turret ventilator is visible near the front of the roof, flanked by periscopes. (The Tank Museum, Bovington, Dorset)

An overhead view of a Staghound III with early, bolt-on engine covers. The roof of the Staghound III's turret was considerably modified from that of the Crusader III: the Crusader's left hatch was retained, but the right hatch was welded shut, a cutout was made in part of that hatch and the roof, and a new, slightly raised hatch was fashioned. This vehicle lacks a right hatch door. Note also the periscope added to the rear of that hatch. (The Tank Museum, Bovington, Dorset)

Top left: Two troopers sit atop a Staghound III. The upper storage box on the side of the hull has a vertical, rather than a tilted, outer face. (12MD Museum, Brandon, Manitoba)
Top right: This Staghound III has a late-type rear deck with hinged engine covers and swiveling lifting eyes. There appear to be nonstandard covers over the muffler flanges and/or mufflers. (12MD Museum, Brandon, Manitoba) **Above left and right:** 12th Manitoba Dragoons crewmen pose with their Staghound III. (Sgt. George Hoffman)

The turret of a Staghound III undergoing restoration in Denmark by the Jyske Dragonregiments Veteran Panser Forening is on a chain hoist. The rear of the vehicle is in the background; the left engine compartment door is open to the far left. (Flemming Hendriksen and Jesper Wilhelmsen)

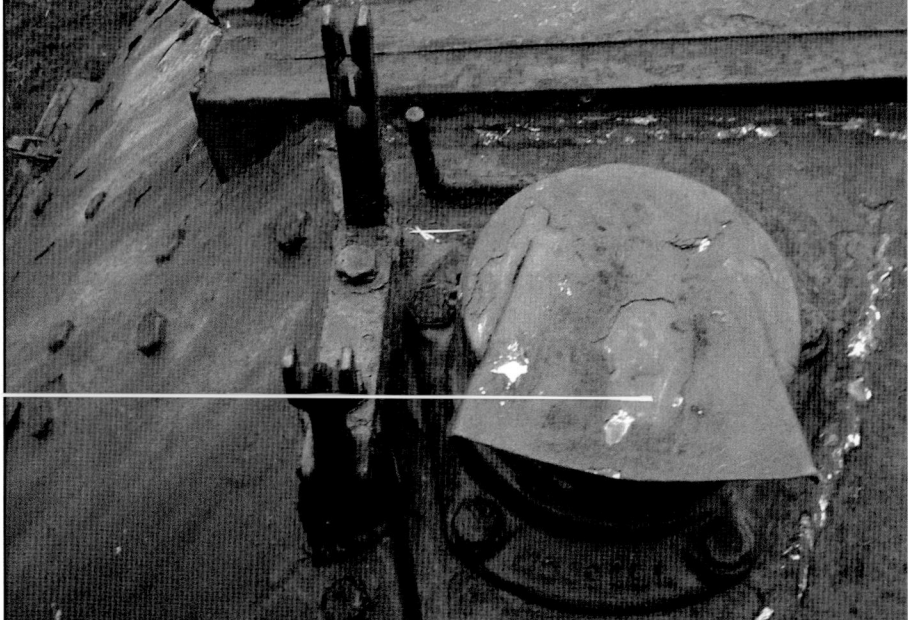

Left: As viewed from the turret roof, the aperture for the smoke grenade launcher is at the lower right. Note the welded shut assistant driver's hatch. **Top right:** In this view from the front of the Mk III turret, the three periscopes and the raised coaming around the commander/loader's hatch are in view. **Above right:** Note the vane sight installed in front of the commander/loader's hatch, which was used for roughly aiming the turret. (Flemming Hendriksen and Jesper Wilhelmsen)

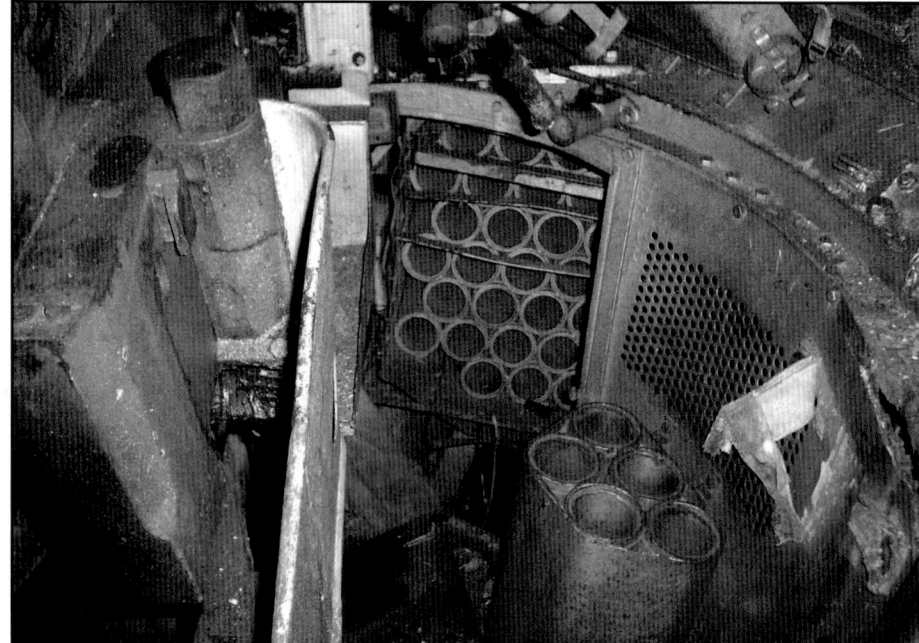

Top left: A close-up of the front of the gunner's periscope, with part of the turret ventilator visible to the left. **Top right:** A view of the right side of the interior of the Mk III turret, with the breech of the main gun to the left and the ammunition storage bin in the former assistant driver's compartment visible through the turret basket door. **Above left:** To the right of the driver's seat of this Staghound Mk III under restoration is the 6 pdr ammunition box. **Above right:** With the turret removed, its traversing gear and its deteriorated basket are visible, including a seat and, at bottom center, the collector ring. (Flemming Hendriksen and Jesper Wilhelmsen)